walked in your shoes. It is even more valuable when it is with no agenda other than to provide a thoughtful per- from an individual who has great experience to share. In *nder,* Maynard Webb shares the gift of his incredible ex- . This is much more than a book that you read once and . *Dear Founder* is a playbook to help you plan and it is a that you can refer back to as you run into new situations e journey of leading your company."

—Alfred F. Kelly Jr., CEO of Visa

rd Webb always gets the big picture to what it takes to be sful—he goes where there is disruption, sees opportunity, arks tremendous growth and success. *Dear Founder* helps reneurs and leaders look through this lens with him as s manage the nitty-gritty you experience day to day in the hes." —Jerry Yang, cofounder and former CEO of Yahoo!

I had this book when I got started at Sun Microsystems. I'm working on some very important startups: my four sons. will be on the top of their reading list—as it should be for y budding economic superstar contributing to the private or."

—Scott McNealy, cofounder and chairman of Wayin, cofounder of Sun Microsystem (WIN Affiliate)

Dear Founder, Maynard Webb reminds us we're not born an trepreneur; we learn to be one. Being an entrepreneur is not ly about starting a company; it's a state of mind."

—Beth Axelrod, head of Global Employee Experience, Airbnb (WIN Affiliate)

n lucky enough to be one of the founders who can call Maynard Webb a mentor and advisor. *Dear Founder* perfectly captures

D0436256

"*Dear Founder* is going to be a 'm
thinking of or contemplating a star
extraordinary resource for leaders a
industry." —Howard Schul
and Cl

"Maynard architected much more t
helped us build operations that could
could be proud of. Now, with *Dear F*
to his wisdom and advice. This book
for anyone running a company today."
—Meg Whitman, CEO o
Hewlett Pac

"*Dear Founder* is an indispensable handb
every stage of their journey."
—Marc Benioff, chairman

"The title of the book is *Dear Founder,* bu
practices are incredibly relevant for a CEO
ization. In today's environment of rapid ch
disruption, we all lead startups and should b
'day one,' with a need to operate with a fou
insightful, empathetic, and practical wisdom
the breakthrough ideas one would receive whe
with a trusted mentor. It is a must-read for any
—Brad D. Smith, chairman

"Being a CEO, regardless of the size of the compa
job. A great gift to a CEO is sound, pragmatic cou

who has
provided
spective
Dear Fo
perience
move o
resourc
along t

"Mayna
succes
and sp
entrep
well a
trenc

"I wis
Now
This
ever
sect

"In
en
on

"I'
W

Maynard's wisdom as he guides you every step of the way along the entrepreneur's journey." (WIN CEO and Affiliate)

—Tien Tzuo, CEO of Zuora and bestselling author of *Subscribed*

"I've had a great career in technology, and nothing was as impactful on my leadership style as the three years I sat next to Maynard. Our discussions about creating companies with cultures of meritocracy, the future of work, leadership styles, acquihires, and the benefits of enterprises and startups continue to influence many of the decisions I make every day. With this book, everyone has access to Maynard's unparalleled wisdom and strong mentorship, and I'm certain they too will see the benefit."

—Jeremy King, CTO of Walmart (WIN Affiliate)

"Every entrepreneur can identify with facing difficult challenges. Maynard Webb has seen them all. His hard-earned advice is relevant for business leaders in any industry who want to take their business to the next level."

—J. Frederic Kerrest, Okta Co-Founder, COO and director (WIN Founder and Affiliate)

"Starting a business is an incredibly challenging experience. You don't always have the answers. Maynard Webb shares the wisdom and guidance in those moments that matter the most. He understands your challenges and pushes you to execute with courage, honesty, and humility. Maynard has done this for me and now he can do this for you."

—Andre Haddad, CEO of Turo (WIN CEO and Affiliate)

"Maynard is every entrepreneur's dream investor—supportive, experienced, and always full of valuable insights. His work with everyone from founders to leaders of Fortune 500 companies makes him uniquely positioned to capture the story of the startup from inception to success across a multitude of verticals. His letters are fundamental for anyone who has aspirations to start, and build, a business."

—Adam Foroughi, CEO of AppLovin Corporation (WIN Founder)

"I had the tremendous good fortune to meet Maynard while working on a startup called AdMob. Maynard was on the board, and I was learning how to build and lead an engineering team under the demands of hyper-growth. No matter how crazy, Maynard seemed to have seen and successfully navigated just about every problem that arose for me and my team during those wild days. Without Maynard's wisdom and wealth of experience which he so generously shared and has continued to share with me over the past many years, my job would have been so much harder. I always wondered how we could scale Maynard so that more entrepreneurs and leaders could benefit from his mentorship. *Dear Founder* is a huge step in that direction."

—Kevin Scott, CTO of Microsoft (WIN Affiliate)

"When things go wrong, business leaders and founders seek Maynard Webb. He delivers a powerful cocktail of compassion & brutal honesty."

—Jim Goetz, Partner at Sequoia Capital

Dear Founder

Also by Maynard Webb

Rebooting Work: Transform How You Work in the Age of Entrepreneurship

Dear Founder

Letters of Advice for Anyone Who Leads, Manages, or Wants to Start a Business

Maynard Webb
with Carlye Adler

St. Martin's Press
New York

 Printed in the United States of America. For information, address St. Martin's Press, 175 Fifth Avenue, New York, NY 10010.

www.stmartins.com

Library of Congress Cataloging-in-Publication Data

Names: Webb, Maynard, 1955– author. | Adler, Carlye, author.
Title: Dear founder : letters of advice for anyone who leads, manages, or wants to start a business / Maynard Webb, with Carlye Adler.
Description: New York : St. Martin's Press, [2018] | Includes index.
Identifiers: LCCN 2018013472 | ISBN 9781250195647 (hardcover) | ISBN 9781250202505 (international sold outside the U.S. subject to rights availability) | ISBN 9781250195654 (ebook)
Subjects: LCSH: New business enterprises. | Leadership. | Entrepreneurship.
Classification: LCC HD62.5 .W4198 2018 | DDC 658—dc23
LC record available at https://lccn.loc.gov/2018013472

Our books may be purchased in bulk for promotional, educational, or business use. Please contact your local bookseller or the Macmillan Corporate and Premium Sales Department at 1-800-221-7945, extension 5442, or by email at MacmillanSpecialMarkets@macmillan.com.

First Edition: September 2018

10 9 8 7 6 5 4 3 2 1

We originally wrote these letters—and this book—as a gift for our founders. We're inspired every day by the opportunity we have to help make founders more successful and to help great new technologies reach the world. We also know that creating a vibrant company is incredibly hard to do. This book is for those who have the courage to do it.

Contents

Foreword

I wish I had this book on my desk for the past forty years.

Thankfully, Maynard Webb has been my friend and counsel for the last twenty.

We met when I was a member of eBay's board of directors, from 1998 to 2001. This was also a unique period in American business. The mid- to late-nineties were exciting times to be an entrepreneur. Everyone, it seemed, had a brilliant business idea and billions of investor dollars flowed into countless startups.

Unfortunately, the indiscriminate influx of capital masked the true difficulty of starting a company. Because it was easy to throw money at problems, the period also was one of hubris, when many founders and business leaders became overconfident in their abilities to build great, enduring companies.

When the internet bubble burst, the day-to-day realities of running a business, especially a startup, could no longer be covered up or ignored. Leaders were suddenly forced to make tough choices and wade through complex challenges, such as how to raise money in a down market, how to spend the funds they had wisely, how to scale without sacrificing core values, how to inspire deflated employees, as well as how to deal with poor performers, new competitors, crisis, and failure.

Today, we can learn a lot from that era.

For one, leadership is always easier when the wind is at your back, but much harder in the headwinds. That's why humility is so vital for founders, entrepreneurs, and even seasoned CEOs. None of us have all of the answers all of the time. We must have the confidence to acknowledge this, and to consistently seek out and consider wise counsel.

I should clarify that I am not the original founder of Starbucks. I bought the company with investors when it had six stores in Seattle in 1987. But now that the company has grown into a global business, I still consider myself an entrepreneur, always in pursuit of innovative ways to bring people together and improve the quality of life for those in communities around the world. This passion is one many entrepreneurs share, and is especially relevant today.

All of us find ourselves in another era of exciting, unprecedented change that demands thoughtful attention and fresh approaches to problems in all corners of society, from healthcare and education to transportation and communication.

Answers and creative ideas will come not only from bold government leaders, but those in the private and nonprofit sectors. For the best new products and services to take hold, they must be guided to market by people who possess enough humility to know what they do not know so they may build sustainable, values-based organizations that continue to raise capital, attract talent, meet high performance standards, and grow.

This is why *Dear Founder* is so timely and valuable. Your ideas and your organization may indeed be original, but many of the management, operational, financial, and personal leadership questions you have today are not new. Generations of smart people have tackled the same or similar issues, and these recurring quandaries are addressed with candor in the pages that follow.

The author, my friend Maynard, has at one point navigated these problems himself or helped countless others do so, including me. He remains one of the wisest leaders I know, with an intelligence that approaches business and entrepreneurship through a rare mix of strategy and humanity. I have learned much from him over the years, and am so pleased he has written this book to share his experience and wisdom.

Maynard also understands that entrepreneurs take their work especially personally. Because we have a heightened need to solve problems quickly, he has organized his advice by the questions we inevitably ask in the day-to-day struggles of leadership and growing a business. In this way, *Dear Founder* is as effective and efficient as calling the smartest person you know for advice the moment you need it.

He and I want you to succeed. More than ever, the world needs innovative, honest, empathetic, capable leaders to bring compelling ideas, products, and services to fruition. Doing so does not require a business degree, but it does demand humility, and the impetus to seek out and listen to wise counsel, at every stage of the journey.

So let this book be your mentor and role model, coach and counselor, confidant and friend. Come to it with your questions and your fears, as well as an open mind. Do so, and I believe that you will be one step closer to achieving your own dreams.

Onward,

Howard Schultz,
former Executive Chairman and Chief Executive Officer
of the Starbucks Coffee Company

Introduction

About two years ago my son, Kevin, recommended that I read a blog post on the website Medium about a son whose father left him a box of letters. The father was terminally ill—though the son never knew that until he passed away—and the letters were filled with advice on how to navigate the various rites of passage the boy would face throughout his lifetime. It's a poignant and powerful piece. It also turns out that it was fiction.

Still, Kevin urged me to write my own letters—missives of advice to the founders of our portfolio companies to help guide them as they faced issues throughout the life cycles of their companies. He thought I could help them with the gnarly everyday problems of running a business: when they got in a fight with their co-founder, or when their board was driving them crazy, or when they were afraid their idea wasn't working.

It was a good suggestion. I was routinely offering this kind of advice to the more than eighty-five founders in our investment portfolio at the Webb Investment Network (WIN) and it was hard to find the time to have so many 1:1s. Because so many of our founders faced the same issues—and because they had nowhere else to turn—it made sense to try to codify the advice so we could share it more broadly than in an individual meetings. I got to work on a project we called *Letters to a Founder.*

Our original intent was to write letters to offer guidance and coaching for our founders in the moments that mattered most. I wrote each letter with a specific founder and situation in mind, but since so many of our founders face similar challenges I discovered that the advice and anecdotes were usually relevant for other founders, too. I began to send out letters and requests for new letters poured in.

There were so many topics to cover. What do you do when you miss your quarter? How do you focus on what's most important? What do you do when a key hire leaves? When a topic was outside my area of expertise, we looked to the directors at WIN to contribute advice. But we didn't stop there. The most special part of WIN is that it is a network of affiliates—more than eighty amazing individuals, most of whom I've worked with extensively in the past—who now co-invest alongside me, offering money and also advice to startups. These people have started companies that have gone public, run entire departments at fast-growing companies, and have decades of management and industry experience. We asked these affiliates to contribute letters in their areas of expertise and they wrote invaluable pieces covering situations such as what to do when your startup gets sued, when to structure sales commissions, and how to deal with a competitor that enters your space, among others.

Once we had a few dozen letters, we organized them into a book as a gift for our founders. We worked with a small bookbinder in San Francisco and printed several hundred copies—and in no time at all we ran out of books. Founders wanted to share the letters with their friends and asked how they could get more copies to give to their team or as holiday gifts. I kept on getting in trouble with my team for giving books away. They confiscated my stash. We created a downloadable private copy, but that became outdated quickly. There were always new challenges that came up and I was always writing letters to address them.

While I originally wrote the letters and the book for our founders, I knew that the advice would be applicable to an entire universe of founders I didn't know. There were so many people who faced the same struggles, and I would never have the chance to meet or work with most of them. I get to connect with some of these people through my LinkedIn feature, Ask Maynard, but I wanted to do more.

I also realized that the audience for these letters was much wider than I originally anticipated. While my work is mostly with founders who are involved in technology and seeking venture capital money, and eventually looking to go public, there were entrepreneurs in every field, with all sized businesses, who found the advice useful. I shared a book with my physical therapist who said it helped him understand the challenges he was facing in starting his business. His wife was his co-founder and he begged her to read it so that they could learn together. There was just such a vast audience of individuals who were running small businesses—there are 26.8 million small businesses in the United States alone, and more than 600,000 new businesses are started every year here, according to the Small Business Administration—and facing some of the same challenges.

What surprised me more was that there turned out to be people who needed this advice who were not even founders. From Fortune 500 executives to millennials entering the workforce, having a founder's mindset is now seen as an invaluable asset.

Additionally, I've discovered that what founders often need is not just advice about how to raise a seed round or how to pick out the best board members, but also coaching on how to deal with people. They need to know how to manage others and they need to know how to act like leaders themselves. Therefore, many of the letters in this book focus on management and leadership. Because I was an operating executive for Fortune 500 companies (IBM, Quantum, Gateway, Bay Networks, eBay) for much of my career, much of my wisdom is gained from working with big companies. Additionally, in my role as a board director I advise many business leaders who are not founders. Many of these letters address challenges they face and were written with them in mind—but they are also relevant to many others.

I wrote this book as a way to scale beyond my network. We only work with about eighty-plus companies, but there are so many more people who think like a founder and need this advice. Maybe you are an entrepreneur eyeing a move to Silicon Valley, or maybe you are a small business owner with a shop in town, or maybe you were just promoted to be a manager at your company. In any case, there's something in this book for you.

This book is intended to be a guide, and the letters are written to offer guidance when you encounter turbulence. Topics are outlined to offer advice at the defining moment you need it most. Just jump to the letter you need when you miss your quarter, when you receive negative publicity, or when you need inspiration. It's not necessary to read this book from start to finish, although of course you may, and many people do, as they may be curious for another perspective about what they might have already conquered or wish to see what lies ahead. The book follows the trajectory of a company's life cycle. I've been inspired as the companies we work with have grown and organized the book to follow the process: getting started, getting to relevance, getting to scale, and getting to legacy. Of course it must be stated that this process is ridiculously hard.

Right now we are in the midst of a Golden Age of entrepreneurship that is fueled by all segments of the population. College students are signing up for entrepreneurial courses in record numbers. Individuals over the age of sixty-five are creating more companies every year. Record numbers of downsized professionals are starting their own ventures. Of those individuals who have not yet taken a leap into entrepreneurship, research reveals that many of them are actively dreaming about it.

Success, though, is hard to achieve. With each phase of company development, the success stories become fewer and fewer. While a massive number of companies get started, only about 30% of them will go on to raise a Series A round of funding, and from there only 50% them will get to a Series B. That number will continue to halve with every additional step.[1] A very small number of companies will go public, and even fewer will leave a legacy.

Writing these letters and compiling them into a book for you has been a labor of love, and I hope these letters help make you better and help your teams achieve their dreams. Unlike the fictional father who inspired this project, these letters are not meant to be the last word we have on these subjects (or any subjects). If you need guidance on topics that are not here, please reach out to us at maynardwebb.com where my network and I will continue to post new letters and answer your questions.

Wishing you luck and cheering you on.

1. Rowley, Jason D. "The Startup Funding Graduation Rate Is Surprisingly Low." Mattermark, September 28, 2016.

PART I

GETTING STARTED

1

The Early Days

WHEN YOU WANT TO START A COMPANY

Dear Founder,

Really?

Why do you want to do this? I hope it's not because it's the cool thing to do . . . it's easy to become an entrepreneur, but it's way harder to become a successful entrepreneur!

These days it seems everyone wants to be an entrepreneur. People become enamored with the idea of pursuing their own passion and being in control of their own destinies. Yet that's a romanticized notion of what really happens.

I hate to be the bearer of bad news, but most entrepreneurs fail. It's not just the statistics that show us this; it's also common sense. It's very hard to turn an idea into reality, and even harder to turn that new reality into something of great significance.

Sure, we know the breakout stories—those A+ ideas that took off from the beginning, like Facebook, Google, or eBay. Yet the fact is that these companies are very rare. Oftentimes, the world is not ready for a new idea and the majority of companies don't get traction. Intrepid entrepreneurs go back to the drawing board and pivot, but that maneuver is not representative of the reality of startups. Most companies fall in a middle space—there's some traction, but the flywheel isn't spinning, and you're not sure if the idea will scale. This uncomfortable middle place is what I call a "tweener" and it's a dangerous place to be.

So, you're still keen on starting something? A number of questions for you:

- **What are your motives?** Are you in this for money or impact? You must know what you're really chasing; otherwise, you'll never find it.
- **Do you have an idea that you are deeply passionate about?**

This question is perhaps the most important one. If you pursue your idea, you will likely be waking up every morning of the next two to ten years touting its value not just to your employees, but also to your customers, to your friends, to your family, and to your significant others. Even if you are the first to realize the concept, large entities and new startups will be quick on your heels. There are thousands of opportunities for new businesses—pick one that's right for you.

- **Do you have a co-founder who will join you?** If not, open the letter "When you are selecting a co-founder" next.
- **Do you have the right team to take this on?** Often, the best teams have spent much of their time working together before, through good times and bad, with each member bringing something distinctive to the table.
- **Are you comfortable with risk?** If you need certainty, being an entrepreneur probably won't make you very happy. At its core, starting a company is a high-risk/high-reward endeavor.
- **Can you afford to live on a small income for years in advance?** You certainly won't get paid handsomely in the beginning. For example, Eddy Lu (co-founder of one of our portfolio companies, Grubwithus, now called GOAT), slept in his car when he started his company.
- **Do you mind working way harder than ever before, and under conditions of much higher stress?** You will wear more hats and have more responsibility than you've ever had. You will also be responsible for the well-being of your team, and the satisfaction of your customers.
- **Do you really want to go for years without great benefits, long vacations, work-life balance, etc.?** There is no balance when starting a startup!
- **Do you need outside validation?** If you need a pat on the back, you may not make a good entrepreneur. You need faith in yourself; you cannot rely on others to keep you going.

Find strength in your passion for the idea and your interest in changing the world.

- **How do you deal with rejection and how much grit do you have to pick yourself up and make something out of nothing?** Know that conviction is required. You'll get nothing but pushback all day long, from everyone you encounter—investors, people who use the product or service, people who are testing it out. You cannot get depressed at hearing "no" or that your idea is "stupid." Instead, you need to be inspired by it.

If you can get through all of my skepticism and doubt, and you still are game for trying, here's my advice:

- **Go for it!** There's nothing more fun than creating something out of ether.
- **Keep your eyes wide open.** Determine the amount of time and resources that you are willing to commit to this project. For example, "I'm going to self-fund up to $100,000 and spend six months testing out my idea," or "I'm going to commit to this idea/company for the next five years without thinking about anything else."
- **Make sure your family and friends are supportive of the risk you will take.** There will be many sacrifices all around, and everyone needs to be on board and understand the road ahead. Otherwise, you may end up with more pain in your personal life than you desire.
- **Can you dip your toe in the water?** Can you start trying to do this while you are still employed? I did this when I created WIN, and my early experience encouraged me to transition more quickly.
- **Once committed, don't look back and wonder; put all of your energy into making this successful.** Pledge total focus

and commitment. Building a company is a long-term proposition. Knowing that you're making a commitment for a decade will give you the perspective you need to make it through the tough moments.

Is it difficult to be an entrepreneur? Absolutely. But it's also fun (and terrifying at same time). It's just like caring for a baby. You are excited about the idea, but there are times when everything turns to poop and you're constantly up in the middle of the night. You are going to be tired and frustrated, but also fulfilled beyond anything you could have imagined.

If that sounds right, you are ready to handle the ups and downs of being an entrepreneur. If not, it's not your time to have a startup—after all, unlike with a baby, you can't hire a nanny to do the work for you.

All the best,

Maynard

WHEN YOU ARE SELECTING A CO-FOUNDER

Dear Founder,

Well, since you opened this letter, it seems like you don't have a natural co-founder in mind.

That's okay. I'll offer some suggestions below on how to find and vet someone, but you'll need to first accept that the magic formula to finding a co-founder is more complex than it seems. When it works, the equation looks like this: $1 + 1 = 3$.

You probably already know that building a business is lonely and hard work. It's easier (but still not easy) with the right partner by your side. Having the right co-founder increases your chance of success, enabling you to go further faster. A few reasons why:

- **Having a partner increases your commitment level.** Making a commitment to someone increases your chance of following through with your goals. It forces you to answer to someone. Having someone hold you accountable is especially important in the beginning, before you've taken any money from investors (other than perhaps your friends and family, who tend not to pay too much attention to the speed of progress).
- **A co-founder can help keep you sane.** The days are filled with roadblocks and disappointments and often end with self-doubt. It can be easier to stop doing this work than to continue through with it. A partner who shares the same passion and who is driven by the same goals, vision, and values will offer the appropriate encouragement and pressure to stay at it. You can't underestimate the value of having a sounding board, therapist, and cheerleader on deck.
- **A co-founder enables you to do more.** A great product person needs a great engineer. A great visionary needs a great

operations czar. When I created WIN and Everwise, I did them with co-founders. In both instances I needed someone who was willing to run the organizations full-time. In both cases I also found having someone with me made the whole dialogue richer and the end result better. Different individuals bring different skills to the table, as well as different perspectives. Co-founders often push each other in their respective disciplines—and this interaction drives overall results. Look for someone with skills and abilities that you don't have and that will complement—and extend—your own.

You have to pick the right partner because the danger of making a mistake throws the entire equation off balance. With the wrong partner, 1 + 1 can equal 0. So, how do you find the right person? A few tips:

- **Consider someone you know.** The best of all worlds is finding a co-founder whom you already know, someone you have worked with before, and someone you trust and know inside and out. Greatness often happens with someone you have already collaborated with. Consider how Jerry Yang and David Filo hacked together in school before building Yahoo! My co-founder at WIN worked with me at LiveOps and my co-founder at Everwise was an affiliate in my investment network. I knew the magic that could be created with these people.
- **Determine what they add to the equation.** You'll want to select someone with complementary skills (e.g., sales/marketing vs. engineering).
- **Get to know them deeply, and spend lots of time together.** Founding a company is a big deal. You might want to work your way into it and see if it is working. At Everwise, co-founders Mike Bergelson, Colin Schiller, and I in-

vestigated the market and spent a lot of time collaborating before we turned it into a formal endeavor. You have to review how the collaboration is working along the way. Do you crave more time together, or wish it had ended earlier? Does this person bring you energy, or take it away? Early interactions with negative chemistry are not going to get better over time.

- **Find references upfront (and back channel).** The more of a 360-degree view you can achieve, the better your perspective will be. Look at the references they give you, but also speak to people they did not give you as a reference, but who may have worked with them or know them in a more personal capacity. (Also, if they've given you a reference and it's not strong, that's a big red flag.) Ask others about how they handle pressure and good and bad situations. You'll also want to learn what motivates them.
- **Is this the one person that you would seek out to solve the deepest problem?** If you are choosing them out of convenience, maybe you need to spend more time looking for a great partner. Look for someone who has the deepest experience in the universe in your topic area. Maybe this person is someone you've worked with before, as was the case with Andy Ludwick and Ron Schmidt who created magic together at SynOptics. Maybe it's someone you've never worked with before, as was the case with Marc Benioff and Parker Harris at Salesforce.
- **Make sure you are aligned.** People want different things in life. Just as you need to discuss what you want before entering a marriage (e.g., Do you both want kids?), you must discuss what you want for the company—and reconcile any differences. Some people want a change-the-world business, while others want a lifestyle business. Neither is bad, but they are different. Figure out your values and motivators

upfront and discuss the following: How do you think about work-life balance? Compensation structure? How big do you want to grow this endeavor? What's the ideal exit strategy?

- **Determine roles and equity structure.** Are you looking for an equal partner (e.g., 50/50 split)? Or, are you looking for a more junior co-founder? Think ahead about what you want your working relationship to be like. Are you okay being challenged? Are you willing to have this be totally equal in terms of equity even if only one person is the CEO? There are pros and cons and ramifications to each of these decisions and they are long-standing.

There are few decisions that you will make in your company's life—including picking the right co-founder, deciding on the right board members, and choosing a strategy—that have the potential to make more of an impact than any other choices. Take your time and make sure you potentially are making the right decisions. If all goes well, these decisions will be with you for decades.

All the best,

Maynard

Do I even need a co-founder?

Perfectly paired co-founders are as legendary as Hollywood power couples and beloved bandmates. The conventional playbook says that you receive more by working together than you give up by splitting all of the winnings. Yet is the calculus that simple? The good and the bad of starting a business alone versus with co-founders:

THE PROS OF FLYING SOLO

- **You retain full ownership of all upsides.** There are much stronger financial incentives should the company be successful.
- **You have the opportunity to completely define your company culture and business model.** Going at it alone forces you to gain experience across all aspects of the business, such as hiring, selling, managing a technical team, fundraising. You'll fast-track a well-rounded education.
- **Decision-making is easy.** You make all of them!
- **You started this business with a vision—and you'll get to keep control of it (at least in the early stages before you have a board).** You are the only one calling the shots on evolving the idea, hiring the initial team, raising money, and building the corporate structure.

THE CONS OF BEING ON YOUR OWN

- **Even if you have a team in place, it can be lonely to be the only founder and to bear all of the responsibility exclusively.** The early days of starting a company can be very difficult—rejections are common and losses happen—and it can be beneficial to have people who are in it with you.

- **You lose the benefit of having a debating partner with nearly the same vested interest as you.** The toughest decisions in business often involve weighing different sets of opportunities against one another. Having several voices can encourage rich discussions and can bring new ideas to light. With fewer founders, there are also fewer resources to leverage—each founder will vastly increase the network that can be tapped for key efforts such as recruiting.
- **You sacrifice the opportunity to gain a partner with complementary skills in areas that you don't have.** Often the best product leaders are not the best developers or salespeople. Having multiple founders can encourage specialization and playing to each individual's strengths. Different individuals bring different skills to the table, as well as different perspectives, and different roles.
- **There's someone to answer to.** Co-founders keep each other honest. A bit of healthy competition can be useful. Co-founders often push each other in their respective disciplines—and that drives overall results.

While there are always exceptions to the rule, we believe that there are greater benefits to collaborating with co-founders. We often find two founders with complementary skill sets to be the best formula for a successful startup. The more self-sufficient an early founding team is (in areas such as tech, sales, marketing), the less dependent it will be on early hires and the more control it will exert over its destiny.

WHEN A CO-FOUNDER ISN'T PULLING THEIR WEIGHT

Dear Founder,

Selecting a co-founder is one of the most pivotal decisions you've made to date. You went in hoping for a decades-long partnership. You've admired what the legendary co-founders—Bill Hewlett and David Packard, Steve Jobs and Steve Wozniak, Larry Page and Sergey Brin—achieved, and you wanted the same destiny.

The reality is that even these celebrated partnerships hit serious and sometimes insurmountable roadblocks. You're not alone.

Still, that doesn't matter now. It's upsetting when you're working your tail off and someone else isn't as engaged or committed. This situation has to get resolved—immediately. First, as always, you need to investigate what's happening to understand what's behind the change in commitment. Suddenly not pulling one's weight is a symptom of something else.

Is the lack of effort new?

Was your co-founder once a tiger, and now is a mouse? Was your co-founder once a "step on the brakes" person that always had to be told to slow down, but now things are not happening at the same pace and you need to tell them to "step on the gas"?

If so, what has changed? Is this something related to work, or not?

Find out why this behavior is happening now.

Do this investigation with an air of wonder. Approach the situation in exploration mode. Never open with criticism; that will not lead to a great resolution.

At one company, we had an issue with someone who suddenly began to behave very differently. Whereas he was once very reliable, now he was flakey and unavailable. We soon learned that he was going through a difficult divorce. The stress of this personal crisis was affecting him at work, but it was neither work-related nor fixable. In this case, we discussed the situation and called out the behavior, and we also gave him some space—but not so much space that he could drag the team down for a long time.

Of course there can be other reasons, too, that are similarly out of your control: someone's health, an issue with a family member, or a myriad of personal reasons that are affecting performance at work. Sadly, a co-founder or key employee may need to step away to care for their own health. In such extreme cases, running a startup and managing their own care are incompatible, and the most important thing is for them to focus on healing.

There's another scenario we sometimes see happen, a reduction in motivation after achieving a certain level of success. At one company, we had an interesting phenomenon: some of the folks who had been there before the IPO suddenly made hundreds of millions. They came into work in their Ferraris at 10 a.m. and left by 3 p.m. No longer motivated by earning more money, they "quit on the job." That's something that must be addressed—and stopped.

If there's no personal crisis looming in the backdrop and no jackpot influencing the behavior, it's time to figure out: Is this something within your control? Ask yourself: *What do I own? What do they own?*

Unfortunately, it's all too common that a conflict in personalities has arisen. There may be bad blood due to any number of reasons, disconnects on strategy or culture, economic inequity, etc. This leaves one of the founders disgruntled and difficult to get along with. Both of you have come to dislike each other. Now what?

It's up to you to find out:

- Is there resentment over ownership? Hopefully not, as that should have been resolved from the onset, but sometimes there's a lingering bitterness that turns into an untenable situation. And this leads to a tricky question: How do you handle the resolution of ownership if your co-founder is slowing down, yet you are still there night and day?
- Is there an issue because someone gets too much credit?
- Is this an issue over strategic direction?

Having a successful marriage is hard. It requires dialogue and communication all the time. The co-founder relationship requires the same attention and care:

- **Find the source of the problem.** And quickly figure out if it's recoverable or not.
- **Call the co-founder out on any bad behavior.** It is unacceptable to not pull your weight or to engage in dysfunctional behavior.
- **Bring in coaching or help from an outside adviser.** You need to do everything within your power to try to save this relationship.
- **Think of everyone involved.** A little time off for someone carrying a stressful situation to work may do them some good, but you have to be mindful of the other people at the company and how they might view this special treatment. Everyone knows the difference between strong and poor performers, and they are counting on the leaders to set an example and fix the issue.
- **Get the board's input.** The board has seen this movie many times and they will have suggestions. They may offer creative solutions they've seen work in the past, such as formally changing the equity structure to reflect the reduced engagement.

- **Figure out a fair way to move on.** If you decide that the partnership is not going to work, move with dignity and grace on that decision. Do not assign blame. Don't disparage each other.
- **Sometimes, a solution to this tension may involve recasting the role of your co-founder.** In my experience, it's extremely rare for both co-founders to scale equally along with their business over the long-term, as your job changes so dramatically with each new level of company growth. Your co-founder's current management role might become something they do not enjoy or are not very good it. Reassigning roles in the company is a delicate process, but ultimately this can result in a much better outcome for all parties.
- **Determine, "what's life like on other side?"** What skills did your co-founder bring? What needs to be replaced? It's likely someone else has stepped up already. My best moments have been seeing what people can do when you give them an opportunity. Think about who can take on new responsibilities and help through the challenge of losing a critical player in the company.

The rift you are experiencing is painful, and it can be as difficult as going through a divorce. However, the difference is that if you don't stay together, this doesn't end with a joint custody agreement. One of you will have to give up the baby. That's terribly hard. I'm sorry and I wish you better days ahead.

All the best,

Maynard

WHEN YOU NEED TO RECRUIT

Dear Founder,

You need great people! Unfortunately, most executives and companies stink at recruiting, which is incredibly unfortunate because it's so crucial.

Think about it: What makes great companies great? People. It's all about people, yet we often don't know how to put our best foot forward when recruiting.

When you start out, you're probably only looking to hire a few people—not an army. With a small team, it's critical to get only the very best players. However, too many founders often see this as limiting and intimidating. This fearful thinking needs to be changed: Founders need to play offense instead of defense.

Don't ever think that you are working from a disadvantage—that what you are working on isn't great enough to attract top talent. Instead, understand that you are working from a position of strength. It's all about attitude. Operate from a mind-set that demonstrates that what you are building is very rare and special. Think about how you are offering a once-in-a-lifetime ground-floor opportunity to those who are qualified to participate. It's like having front row seats at the Super Bowl or *Hamilton*: You only have two open seats—which of your friends will be lucky enough to be invited?

A few rules to help you rethink about recruiting:

- **Always be recruiting—even when you don't have openings.** At eBay, I was always looking for talent and generally had one or two "ready-now" recruits I could woo for any critical position that worked for me. I learned this from Meg Whitman, who knew the company was growing quickly and therefore would hire people whom she had no jobs for, knowing that she'd have a job for them in the future. Full disclosure: Sometimes this created tension because they wanted to do something, but there wasn't a well-defined role for them when they joined and they had to focus on "special projects." But more often than not, they soon landed big operating roles.

- **Own the process.** Recruiting is not just someone else's job. You need to invest your own focus and time. When I was at LiveOps, an exec at one of our biggest customers suggested I meet with Mike Bergelson, a talented entrepreneur who had recently sold his company to Cisco. I sent Mike several emails inviting him to get together to speak. When he finally responded, I made a pitch for him to join us, but he gave me the Heisman. Nevertheless, we agreed to stay in touch. When I founded WIN, Mike expressed that he wanted to join as an affiliate—something against the "house rules" as we had never worked together—but he agreed to do some consulting for one of our portfolio companies and we agreed to make an exception and let him join WIN. Not long after, I started talking with him about my idea for a mentoring service and within a few months he became the co-founder of Everwise. The lesson to that long story: You always have to be on the lookout for talent you resonate with—you can't just wait for what HR or someone on your team might bring you.
- **Treat people well throughout the process and make sure they have an experience they enjoy.** Being superior or arrogant will hurt you. Yes, you get to make the decision on whether someone will be asked to join or not, but there's no reason to have them be embarrassed or insulted by the process. One of our Founders-in-Residence told us that she had a bad recruiting experience at a company, which she then told her friend about. When that friend later got called for

the same job, she wouldn't even interview. That company didn't even get a chance with her because of the way they treated someone else! Treat everyone with dignity and respect, and give them helpful feedback. You want everyone to leave feeling good and wishing they get the chance to come back sometime later. (We practice what we preach at WIN, too, where we have to say "no" often, but we aim to do so in a very friendly way. Because of that, we've often had other deals referred to us by the same folks we've said no to.)

- **Do the reference checks yourself, and personally say no to people.** Don't hide behind the people or the process. Maybe outsourcing these pieces of the process is more efficient and it gets you out of giving bad news, but it's not thoughtful. Gain credibility by treating prospective hires like human beings.
- **Don't look for people who are just like you.** Look for people with the skills you need and the types of people who bring diverse perspectives and will contribute to your culture.

  - **Don't be swayed by big names.** Just because somebody works for a great company, it doesn't mean that they are great or will be right for your startup. There's a big difference between being on the bus at a great company and actually driving the bus. There are also great talents out there who don't always work for brand-name companies.
  - **Pay extra attention to those with a "chip on their shoulder."** The best hires often have something to prove, and are motivated by a profound desire to excel in their jobs.
  - **Rule out people motivated mostly by money.** If your candidate is focused on a high salary, you should be

questioning whether or not they are the right fit. (Being motivated by equity is a different story as that's tied to performance and demonstrates a belief in the company.)

- **Make your company attractive to potential hires by being the best place to work.** Be the place people are clamoring to join. There's no entitlement for employees anymore, and there's no entitlement for companies. Being the best place to work is not about massages and gourmet food; it's about what was accomplished, what was learned, and how well people are treated.

    - **Have huge aspirations.** Be inspirational with what you are trying to accomplish.
    - **Be humble.** Never stop trying to get better.
    - **Be fun to hang with.** Care about your people. You want to think that yours was the best and most fulfilling job that they ever had. That's never about money; it's about being a part of something meaningful.
    - **Foster a culture of inclusion.** Make sure you are building a place where each member of your diverse and talented team can feel like they belong.

Congratulations on your growth and your need to hire. You are in a good place. And soon, you will be in a better place. Recruit always!

All the best,

Maynard

WHEN YOU NEED TO HIRE A ROCK STAR

Dear Founder,

You should only be hiring rock stars.

We all know that hiring mistakes are costly. Therefore it's best to prevent them . . . but how? What can you do initially to prevent surprises later? While employees with diverse skills and backgrounds are necessary for building a standout company, I find that there are universal attributes great employees tend to share. When I hire, I:

Value an individual with a track record of success. I'm not just looking for someone who was promoted at their last job, and the one before that (though I am also looking for that). I'm looking for success over a long period of time. Ask what they have personally done of significance. See rapid progression in their career as a good sign. Shy away from individuals who want to be assured that the job is easy and that they will be able to ride the work of others to make tons of money (yes, this can come out in interviews).

Look for someone who has a chip on their shoulder and something to prove. It's not perfection you need to prize, or even the balanced resume. You want to hire a person who has something powerful driving them to succeed—someone scrappy who has grit. For example, someone who struggled in school, but who built several successful ventures while there, might very well be the perfect candidate for you. When I recruit, I invariably ask about someone's past as far back as middle school, and I want to know what they spent their time on. I'm looking for a track record of excellence and bandwidth, along with a willingness to take on tough challenges and risks. I've worked with individuals who got straight As in school and did ballet, people who had lemonade stands that did better every summer, and folks who were the first in their families to go to college. And *where* they go to college doesn't always matter. In fact, stats show that most CEOs of the biggest corporations went to state universities or less-known private colleges, not the Ivy League or other elite colleges. Look at someone like Lee Scott, the retired CEO of Walmart who we recruited to the Yahoo! board. We learned about his roots—which included him working making tire molds for $1.95 an hour to pay his way through college, living with his wife and son in a trailer, and starting at Walmart in the transportation department and working his way up—and we found his story to be incredibly inspiring.

Scout for someone who doesn't take no for an answer. Some people see barriers; others see opportunities. The best employees have likely been told they "can't" a lot of times. And yet, they did not let that deter them. Look at education activist Reshma Saujani, the co-founder of Girls Who Code. She was rejected from Yale Law School three times before she transferred in. Later, she ran for public office and lost by a landslide. However, she had the intestinal fortitude to continue to chase her dreams, and she became a role model illuminating the power of bravery over perfection for girls—and everyone—everywhere.

Prize a person with a following. If this individual goes somewhere, will they inspire others to join? Never underestimate the power of someone's ability to recruit; it suggests that this person has built up years of goodwill and trust with others. And, better yet, this often leads to a new infusion of great talent eager to follow this leader wherever they head next.

Pick people who will help you and your culture grow. I learn from people I've worked with in more ways than I can tell you. They have years of experience with different problems, different organizations, and different attitudes. And for CEOs—particularly those who are early in their careers—I can't recommend enough the value of bringing in people who will commit to helping you grow as a leader. Don't eliminate people because they don't seem like a "culture fit" (see the "When you need to hire diverse candidates" letter)—embrace the differences, and stay rigorously focused on the cultural attributes that *actually* define your company.

Finally, just a reminder—hiring anyone requires romancing. No matter how far along your company is, you should remember that you have to be selling what working with you, and working for this company, will be like—and the recruitment process offers an excellent window into this. Don't make your evaluation process so stressful that your candidates make your hiring decision for you. Good luck!

All the best,

Maynard

WHEN YOU NEED TO SET YOUR CULTURE

Dear Founder,

From day one it is important to pay attention to culture. *What is it that you want your company to stand for? What is its purpose? What are its values? How are people treated? What do you think about flexible work hours? Working remotely? How do you address performance issues?* The list is endless. I could go on and on . . .

This may seem overwhelming, but a culture develops whether you design it or not. That's why it's essential to:

1. Have a point of view on what culture you want to have.
2. Live and model what you have stated the culture to be.

Step one, in setting your culture:

- **Don't pick up somebody else's culture and adopt it as your own.** Authenticity matters. You have to develop a point of view on what you want this company to be—otherwise it will not work. Sure, it's said imitation is the highest form of flattery, but when it comes to startup culture, following the fad of the day is a recipe for failure. Copycat cultures—whether it be a me-too foosball table or giving everyone weird job titles with the word ninja in them—will never last. The best way to build a strong culture is to start at the beginning, by paying attention to your values and thinking about what types of practices will celebrate and extend them. A strong culture is a genuine culture.
- **How do you decide what's important?** It starts with asking a series of questions. These questions all have unique answers that can help identify who you are and what your company cares about. Questions like:

- How frugal are you? Josh James, the founder of Domo, wrote a great blog post (www.joshjames.com/2012/04/dont-spend-money/) about why he didn't replace the stained carpet in his new office, saying it was a great reminder to stay "scrappy."
- How do you show you care for and nurture your employees? When I was CEO at LiveOps and the CFO wanted to cut free food, I couldn't allow that to happen because it would send the wrong signal to employees.
- What does your office space look like? At eBay, I was shocked when I found out I'd be working in a cubicle, but then I realized Meg Whitman did, too, and this arrangement exemplified the open and collaborative style that defined the workplace.
- Do you have a learning environment? What are the opportunities to receive mentorship and personal growth? Facebook has a "hackamonth" where employees take a month off to pursue a project they are passionate about. Bain allows employees in their third year to take a six-month "externship" where they work in a different office or for a different organization.
- Do people have to come into the office, or can they work from home? At WIN, we value outcomes over face time and we allow people to work from wherever they want.
- What working hours are expected? At Salesforce, employees get seven days a year off to volunteer, signaling that people are at the company to do more than their jobs—they also spend time engaging with their communities.
- How long are people supposed to stay in the office? Google's on-site laundry facility shows that the company encourages employees to spend more time at work than at home.
- How are deadlines managed? At WIN, deadlines are

self-imposed and important; we also have a mandate to be responsive within hours, not days.

- What about pets; are they allowed in the office? I didn't appreciate getting licked on my head by a Labrador retriever who found his way to my cubicle when I was CEO at LiveOps, but his owner appreciated having him there.
- How do you welcome new people? At LiveOps, I welcomed every new hire on their first day. We also brought doughnuts in and asked people to come by and say hello to the new folks. Unfortunately this ignited another cultural phenomenon—the startup twenty-pound weight gain!
- How do you manage departures? In the early days at eBay, we didn't spend much time acknowledging exits. However, we eventually became more enlightened about supporting individuals chasing their dreams elsewhere, and we began to celebrate them on their way out.
- How do you deal with problems? Do you tell people about them early or do you wait? At HP, Meg Whitman implemented a "24 hours to resolve or escalate" policy. At eBay and LiveOps, we had postmortems on each issue encountered. By not making it a blame game, we encouraged people to ask for help early and learn from their mistakes.

- **It is also important to consider how your culture might evolve as the company changes and grows.** What works for three founders doesn't work for fifty people or five thousand. We had to focus on this issue at eBay. We had to figure out how to stay true to our core values while being open to changing some of our practices. (We never lost the focus that we were a marketplace and making our sellers successful was job number one, but we did change some processes. For example, I couldn't make every final decision on new features or every budget line item when we got bigger.)

- One thing to keep in mind is that a culture gets calcified very quickly. At the same time, the world is constantly changing and evolving and cultures must be fluid enough to keep up. Consider, for example, how command and control, once the management style that defined a generation of companies, has largely been deemed uncool. If your culture is not attractive to the next generation of employees and you don't change it, you will lose people.
- Founders should do a culture check every six months with the question: Do we still believe in this? What used to work won't always work, so be ready to change. You have to ask yourself which elements of your culture you will take with you as you grow, and which you will leave behind.

I believe that authenticity is a crucial element of the strongest cultures, as it provides a solid foundation that is also flexible and fluid. This type of culture will never come from copying anyone else's company—it comes from creating something you believe in.

As I said in the beginning, your company will have a culture. You can take overt action to assert and live the culture you want or it will grow organically. It's your choice.

All the best,

Maynard

P.S. I've included an appendix with this letter, which describes the cultures at various organizations I've worked at. I've included this to show you that there's no one formula. Some of these places could not be more different from each other!

APPENDIX

In my personal career I've worked at the following companies and experienced the following cultures:

Strong paternalistic culture. IBM was my first professional work experience and, at one time, I thought I would be a lifer. There was a very hierarchical culture and set of values that made things work for execution, but that didn't cultivate cutting-edge innovation. One of IBM's mantras was, "You can be a wild duck, but you have to fly in formation." Every manager was trained on "dos and don'ts." Employees used to jokingly call this "lobotomy school." There was also emphasis on providing mentoring and feedback. The company invested a lot in its people and did very little external hiring; more often the company promoted from within. It offered great benefits and prioritized making its people feel safe and nurtured. It also expected you to put IBM first—employees moved wherever IBM wanted them to—but as long as you performed, you had a job for life.

The haves and have-nots. When I started at Figgie International I expected that everyone treated people fairly and with respect and dignity, which is what I had experienced at IBM. However, that wasn't the case at Figgie, which was a holding company with a portfolio of forty-two companies, including Caterpillar and Rawlings Sporting Goods. The corporate campus was like a high-end resort with three beautiful brick buildings connected by a tunnel system. Mrs. Figgie picked out the art for everyone's offices—there was no choice or freedom for personal expression. There were basketball courts and an extravagant cafeteria and every director at the company was given a Jaguar, which they also washed for you every week. However, the satellite offices did not receive any of these perks. Figgie would buy these companies, hold them and try to make them more profitable, and then jack the value up and sell to someone else. They really bled these companies. The CFO had to sign every request over a certain amount—and he usually denied them. As a result, everyone in the satellite offices was always nervous they would get fired and there was a constant culture of suspicion and misery outside the corporate campus. I had never experienced such a delta between the "haves" and "have-nots." I left within a year.

Culture of innovation (and hard work). At Thomas-Conrad, we were innovators in the networking space which was exciting. However, people were expected to work crazy hours and there were often firings for minor offenses. Although we were very innovative, it was not a fun or inspiring place to be because of the negative way people were treated.

Political culture that prizes pedigree. Quantum, a disk drive manufacturer, was known for having a good culture, but it was also very political. They made it clear that I was not destined to be a top executive because I didn't have the "look" or the Harvard Business School degree. They executed well and were very cost conscious—every penny mattered.

Wild West culture of innovation and fun. Bay Networks, a router and hub company that was driving the internet, was created by merging an East Coast company called Wellfleet that acted like a West Coast startup, with a West Coast company called SynOptics that acted more like an East Coast company (e.g., they wore suits on Fridays). At this point in my career, I started joining boards and flourishing, and they enabled me and celebrated my success. No one cared about pedigree; they cared that people got things done. The company had high expectations and demanded hard work from everyone, but it was a very loving and fun place.

Culture in flux. When I joined Gateway, it was in the middle of a metamorphosis. There was a brand-new CEO, and they were migrating out of the corporate HQ in South Dakota and moving to San Diego. It was a nice place and they treated me well. I only stayed for a year, so I don't know how the culture evolved and eventually set.

Dual cultures, but both vectored toward success. At eBay, we really had two cultures: one on the business side and one on the product/engineering side. On the business side, there was a lot of striving and competition for the top jobs, although everyone generally executed and communicated professionally. On the tech side, we were good teammates, but I called us the "pack mules" because we knew if we went off the cliff we all went off together. On both sides, there was a culture that prized success based on facts and metrics.

A culture divided. When I joined LiveOps, the teams were very split. Sales and administration were in one camp, and engineering was in another. It was so bad that they had different buildings. We needed more of a unified culture, so we moved to a space where everyone was together, and we did fun things to bring everyone together—paper airplane contests, Thursday night happy hours, Olympic competitions, and other fun events. We got people involved in activities that spanned departments. We had a team of volunteers to create and to manage our foundation, and we also had a team of volunteers called Team LiveOps to help us manage interactions and fun.

A service-driven culture. Marc Benioff cared about philanthropy from the very beginning of founding Salesforce. He pioneered the 1-1-1 model (dedicating 1% equity, 1% of employee time, and 1% of product back into its communities), and has made it front and center for eighteen years at Salesforce. He also focused on innovation and on inspiring a revolution in how software was delivered. He had a relentless focus on execution and used his V2MOM process (a system by which the company defines its Vision, Values, Methods, Obstacles, and Measures) to religiously to monitor and drive it. As a board member at Salesforce for ten years, I have found it marvelous to be a part of this journey and see it evolve. Marc has created a culture of accountability and giving, and he cares about all stakeholders succeeding (not just shareholders)—and we see this in how he fights for equal pay and against discriminatory bills.

A process-oriented culture. When Marissa Mayer became CEO at Yahoo! she radically changed the company by implementing a weekly FYI meeting on Friday afternoons, letting employees have a voice about what were the biggest problems, and systematically knocking them off with her PB&J system (process, bureaucracy, and jam). People appreciate having the opportunity to listen and contribute, especially in tough times.

Culture in progress. Visa is an incredibly sucessful company with a fantastic franchise and brand. Now, it's going through a transition to become even more of a technology company and is opening up its technology for others to use. The payment space is exploding with new entrants and new capabilities. Cognizant of that, Visa is evolving its company and culture. I'm excited to see it develop.

WHEN YOU NEED TO HIRE DIVERSE CANDIDATES

Dear Founder,

I set out to write a letter on the importance of fostering diversity—and how to do so—and found that with every week, and sometimes every day, this issue became more and more complicated. Since I started this letter to you there were new allegations against venture capitalists and startup companies. Silicon Valley, where I live and work—and a place that I love for its commitment to innovation and support of founders—has been exposed as an environment that could be vastly improved for a large percentage of the working population. There's room and reason for all of us to become better at building workplaces that support and celebrate diversity.

I'm not an expert on diversity—not at all—so I decided to consult professionals in this area to help offer advice. What I do know is that ignoring this issue is not an option. And the sooner you can address this as a company the better. Please take this seriously.

Understand why diversity matters.

Sure, we all know that it's the right thing to do. But it's also the right thing to make your company stronger. The performance of your business will be better if you are more diverse because a diverse company is more representative of society as a whole. It better understands its customers, its community, and its purpose. Don't just take my word for it: There's evidence that diverse workplaces perform better. A report from McKinsey & Company indicates that the top racially diverse tech companies are 35% more likely to have financial returns higher than the tech sector's national median. Companies that are more gender diverse are 15% more likely to outperform others.[2]

2. www.mckinsey.com/business-functions/organization/our-insights/why-diversity-matters

I have had the honor and privilege of working directly with two of the best-known female CEOs in technology: Meg Whitman at eBay, and Marissa Mayer at Yahoo! While they are totally different from one another, I've found each of them to be some of the most inspirational, results-oriented leaders with whom I've ever worked. When I step back and think about the ways that companies are subconsciously keeping women from the workplace and from leadership roles, I worry that we're depriving ourselves of a wide pool of potential CEOs in the future. Furthermore, I worry that when my granddaughters see magazine covers of CEOs who look an awful lot like me, they'll think the world of entrepreneurship just isn't for them.

I greatly admire companies that don't ignore this issue because they think it's "too hard" or "not my problem," but instead come up with creative ways to solve for it. Marc Benioff has made it a priority to add significant diversity to the Salesforce board. I've seen how it makes a difference. We have three women and three African American board members, one of whom was the Secretary of State. We have the former ambassador to Japan and we recently added an EU commissioner. We have always had a good and collaborative board during my tenure, but all this added experience makes the dialogue much richer.

This effort to embrace diversity at Salesforce isn't just reflected on the board; it spans across the entire company. It started a few years ago when two women executives came to Marc's office asking if they could take a look at whether the company was paying women less than men. Marc acknowledges that this came as a surprise and even though he was skeptical, he was open-minded and wise enough to commission an internal review. The company leaders looked at the salaries of its global workforce—seventeen thousand employees at the time—and found that although they never intended to pay women less than men, they were. As a result, they added $3 million to the payroll to address the inequities. In 2017, after a year of record growth, they again conducted a pay assessment, increasing the scope of the assessment by evaluating salaries globally, as well as examining both gender and race in the U.S. This resulted in Salesforce spending another $3 million—$6 million total to date—to address any unexplained differences in pay. Marc also created the High-Potential Leadership Program to provide leadership skills to advance women in the workplace. The program has led to an increase in the number of women who were promoted in one year. It also added mandates to make sure that women are being considered for open positions. It didn't stop with closing the gender gap. It made racial diversity a heightened priority and appointed the company's first Chief Equality Officer who reports directly to Marc.

Acknowledge that you will have to work hard to make your company more diverse, but that it's worth it.

Recently I was visiting one of our portfolio companies for our first board meeting. I couldn't help but notice that every new hire was white, young, and male. I asked why and was told, "We know this is a problem, but there just isn't enough pipeline to find other good people now."

The thing is, it is a problem they can fix, and one that they must fix, if they want to ensure the best success for the company. I have to admit, there was a part of me that felt as if I had no business telling the company that they had to focus on diversity. After all, I too am white and male. Yet over the past eight years at WIN, and my forty-year career, we've come to see how crucial it is to be deliberate about making your company inclusive—and doing it early is much, much easier.

I know what it takes to build a great business. I also know that there are plenty of smart and capable and diverse candidates ready for these jobs. We are seeing increased enrollment rates for both women and minorities in tech programs. With 50% of our population being female and nearly 50% in the United States (often overlapping) being racially diverse, the issue is not "pipeline," so that is not a suitable answer. The experts with whom I consulted with said, "lack of pipeline is one of the worst excuses that is used today."

Quantify your problem.

The first step in improving diversity at your company is to measure the breadth of it. How diverse is your hiring funnel? For your current employees, how are they made up across genders, races, religions, region of origin? How does it vary by department, or job role? Across each of these facets, how have you allocated promotions? How has tenure varied? How does pay?

These questions are likely to be *uncomfortable,* and it's likely that even asking them will lead to friction from your team because no one will want to be labeled racist or sexist. Lead through it by acknowledging your own blind spots and by committing to listening and sharing responsibility for the company's shortcomings to date.

Act now, while you are still relatively small.

Businesses have a moral and a fiduciary obligation to make their companies welcoming to different ages, genders, races, and perspectives. Too often, though, I've seen companies kick the can down the road, then try to address the issue when their cultures are already problematic. Masha Sedova, the co-founder of Elevate Security, one of the companies we work with at WIN Labs, helped me further my thinking on *when* companies have to start thinking about this. She told me diversity was such an important value for her company that she prioritizes diverse hires from the beginning—from the very first hire. "People from different backgrounds solve problems in more interesting ways," Masha said. "They come up with solutions that people who are like-minded can't see. The first five hires make a difference."

All companies need to avoid copping out on this big issue. I know it is hard to do, but we need to prioritize making our companies diverse and we must attempt to solve it from the beginning. Experts say diversity must be inculcated into a company early—after fifty people it may be too late.

I have consulted with experts, including Lori Nishiura Mackenzie, executive director of the Clayman Institute for Gender Research at Stanford University; Laura Mather, CEO of Talent Sonar for HR solutions; Masha Sedova, co-founder of Elevate Security; Beth Axelrod, VP of Employee Experience at Airbnb; and legal and HR professionals at eBay, Salesforce, and Visa for advice on how to create a diverse workplace. There are clear steps you should start taking now.

- **Make inclusion and diversity part of your corporate culture.** People will hire based on "fit"—and that often means people like us. Instead, if you build a culture where fit means people who expand who we are, then diversity will be germane to your future success.
- **Think about the company you want to build—not just the one or two spots that are now open.** What matters in the long run? We often get caught in the short-term need to add someone with a functional skill, like project management. We need to also consider how each person adds to the overall diversity of approaches and experiences that will help guide the team through growth and challenges.
- **Prioritize the skills you are looking for before you interview.** Don't use a laundry list. Agree to criteria in advance of seeing candidates, which helps you fairly and effectively evaluate job seekers with different but equal experiences.
- **Disregard unnecessary criteria that can promote bias.** Get rid of anything that may be filtering out quality people—examples might include rigorous expectations of number of years of experience, coming from a set of high-profile universities, or taking a certain curriculum that may not have been available. For example, as I learned from a

presentation Lori delivered, Carnegie Mellon decided high school computer science was not a requirement and increased the percentage of woman from 7 to 42 in five years. You can also add to every job description a disclaimer that explicitly encourages people not *precisely* matching the job spec to apply anyway.

- **Remove subconscious biases from the hiring process.** Write a job spec and test it out to make sure it doesn't only appeal to one group of people, such as men. If we want a talented workforce, we need to look at the whole population not just half! Think about the words you use. "Dominant" and "competitive" are seen as positive traits for men, but as negative attributes for women. Similarly, "competitive," "best of the best," and "fast-paced" appeal more to men and self-select women out. "Ninja" is another one as Japanese ninjas were historically men.[3] Words like "extreme culture" or "exclusive" alienate many people and discourage them from applying. Other words such as "loyalty," "passion," and "collaboration" have been shown to appeal more to women, experts say. It's not that you can't ever use any of these words, but it matters how you use them—make sure that your spec is well-balanced and appeals to all genders equally. Masha used an app called Textio in order to remove gender bias and attract more candidates. Initially she says the req was more male heavy, but they changed the language to make the job requirements more gender neutral and equally attractive to men and women.
- **Look for talent in unlikely or overlooked places.** Masha was looking for ways to reengage moms who were excellent developers but who had left the workforce to raise their kids.

---

3. Peck, Emily. "Here Are the Words That May Keep Women from Applying for Jobs." Huffington Post. June 2, 2015.

She knew there was a talent pool there that desired flexibility beyond what a traditional corporate job could provide, and that this was something she could offer. "I don't see too many parent-friendly examples," she said. "So I decided to build one." She posted job opportunities in daycare centers as a way to target people who had a lot to offer as well as to demonstrate she understood their circumstances and that she could accommodate them. At LiveOps, I found many of our best performing agents to be professional women who valued flexibility, and who had been overlooked by traditional corporate America.

- **Employ a diverse set of interviewers.** Women are much more likely to join a company when they can interact with women who are already there and can testify to a company's commitment to diversity. In fact, one of the biggest deciding factors on whether or not a female candidate accepts a job is if there was a woman on the interview panel. That's because a woman on the interview panel is signaling that the woman candidate can be successful in the workplace, explains Lori. And that woman is more likely to stay if she believes she is aligned with the cultural indicators of success, not just if she has the technical abilities to succeed. Additionally, as a best practice, you should track your interviewers' performances: Who did new hires enjoy engaging with? Who helped to spot people who lasted and succeeded in your company?
- **Reconsider how you define diversity.** Have your eyes open to the many ways we can think about what diversity means. Gender and racial and ethnic diversity may be visible, but ensuring other kinds of diversity such as educational background, geography, economics, family status, disability, sexual preference, gender expression/identity, political inclination, religious affiliation, age, and neurodiversity (people who may

connect the dots differently) is also important. Amy Weaver, general counsel at Salesforce, told me, "Having viewpoints from employees with varied backgrounds reflects the communities we serve and helps us make better decisions."

- **Learn how to value the journey.** We often value recognizable indicators of past success, such as elite schools, or work experience in leading companies. We are less skilled at recognizing unique talent, or those whose journey is possibly longer and less traditional; in many cases, those candidates can demonstrate exemplary grit, resiliency, and creative problem-solving.
- **Use data and facts, not personal preferences, to evaluate candidates the same way.** One study found that white candidates receive 50% more callbacks than black candidates with the exact same resume. Create a standard evaluation system and metrics and use them the same way. Some companies remove names and photos before reviewing them so that they are not aware of race or gender.

It's time to change the thinking on diversity from "a problem" to "an opportunity." By 2022 the workforce is expected to be comprised of 47% women and 40% minorities. If we find a way to appeal to everyone and become a magnet for openness and diversity and inclusion, we will have a stronger company and future.

All the best,

Maynard

WHEN YOU NEED TO CREATE A WORKPLACE OF INCLUSION

Dear Founder,

I've written a letter about the importance of thinking about diversity from the beginning and how to hire diverse candidates, but what about maintaining a diverse culture? Now that you have diverse employees how do you retain them? How do you build a culture of inclusion and belonging?

Once you have a workplace that reflects diversity, you have to do some important work to allow all that talent to thrive—that means creating an environment of inclusion and belonging. Again, I went to a panel of experts more qualified than I for advice on what to do to build this kind of workplace. Here's what they had to say:

- **Examine your culture.** Diversity isn't something you can just hire your way out of. To truly make the workplace more inclusive, evaluate your methods of mentorship and promotion.
- **Support a culture that celebrates inclusion.** Unfortunately, some early stage companies promote a strong "bro" culture, which may make many others feel left out. Embracing diversity means that you may need to change the way you work to accommodate a broad range of people. Employ policies that are equitable for both men and women. For example, paternity leave can go a long way in building empathy for all parents, and helping to build long-term company loyalty. Find ways to keep team members engaged in the company's mission and work, even while they're caring for newborns.
- **Just as you have to be aware of unconscious biases in the hiring process, it's important to mitigate issues like**

unconscious bias through all phases of the employee life cycle. Particular areas to evaluate for inclusiveness are the evaluation process, promotions, and succession planning.

- **Encourage and measure inclusive leadership behaviors.** Be sure that any concerns are taken seriously (i.e., address all red flags).
- **Understand that workplace enhancements to promote diversity and inclusion are also things that would help "traditional" workers, as well as millennials.** This may include promoting work-life balance, demonstrating the meaning in the work, and rewarding loyalty—all of which are important to many types of workers. Find a way to welcome and celebrate everyone and ensure that no one feels isolated. Provide gender-neutral bathrooms and an environment that ensures that employees feel comfortable.
- **Listen.** Consider developing a task force internally, made up of anyone who is committed to seeing your business become more diverse. Meet monthly, and give them latitude to take practices from other companies and employ them. Listen earnestly to their suggestions. And give them the latitude to speak and write about their findings—it may be uncomfortable, but building transparency about your company's interest in improvement will help to win over your next generation of employees. Solicit feedback from your diverse candidates and ask them to score how you are doing and share what they think you can do better.
- **Grow the circle wider.** As you work to become a more modern, inclusive workplace, I encourage you to expand your circle of concern outward. Consider building an internship program with all-female or historically black universities. Adopt a school in an at-risk neighborhood, and send them supplies, bring students into the office, and commit to the school's improvement. Let your employees tell the

story of your company's journey, in the hopes that you inspire others to follow you.

You have taken an important step in hiring diverse candidates and now you must ensure that you establish a culture that will support and foster them. Remember, this work must be constant, and it requires your consistent commitment and nourishment, but with the effort you will see many rewards.

All the best,

Maynard

WHEN YOU ONBOARD AN EXECUTIVE

Dear Founder,

Congratulations! You've reeled in the big fish you were hoping to catch. Now what?

It always seems like *finding* a new executive to join your team is the hard part, but the truth is that successfully integrating them to get the desired outcomes is the real challenge. So, congrats on the hire—now it's time make them successful.

If you're a first-time CEO and you're several years younger than this new professional on your team, you may think, *I hired this person and they are the expert—they'll know what to do.* Please, PLEASE, resist this temptation. I've known many CEOs who've practiced this management approach and I have yet to see it yield great results.

Your job as a manager is to be inspiring, fair, and honest—and to hold people accountable to do their best work. If you do that, you will not go wrong. Don't become intimidated by years of experience, a good reputation, or simple bravado. You're the leader, and while they may be the domain expert, you need to ensure that they (and your company) are successful.

That requires active discussion and engagement on all fronts. A winning recruiting and onboarding strategy entails a lot of dialogue for alignment around:

- What does success look like?
- What is expected of the new executive?
- What authority level does the new executive have? (What authority do they have to hire? What input should they get before they fire anyone?)
- What are the expected behaviors? What is the appropriate style for the culture?

- What do the first ninety days look like?
- What problems will they want to tackle right away? What should be put on hold?
- What is the cadence for check-ins? How often will you be meeting?

I'm a fan of codifying the above in a document so that there's something to go back to and check against. People interpret goals and expectations differently, so this exercise is especially important. I ask the new executive to take the lead and document what we've discussed, and then to let me edit it. We will both frequently check back on the document to see how the role is progressing. I recommend having weekly 1:1s to check in. These meetings also offer an opportunity to provide advice and to solicit input on how you can help them become more successful.

If something is bothering you in your gut, you aren't doing anyone any favors by hiding your concerns. When you articulate your worries, try to do so in a way that's constructive and truth seeking, rather than blaming.

A couple of other points:

- You hired this person for a reason. You therefore know that something needs to be done differently, so expect that there will be some changes. You just need to be aligned about what they are.
- There's a lot to be discussed and imparted, but don't forget that listening goes a long way. Any new executive should be reminded of the importance of listening to the team. I recommend soliciting input about what is going well and where improvement is needed.
- As mentioned earlier, there is likely to be quite a bit of change, and the current team needs to be forewarned about and accepting of the fact that some things might be done

differently under new leadership. If (or, more likely, when) people come to you to complain about the changes, you need to listen, but also route them back to have a transparent discussion with the new executive.

- Don't forget the basics! Do everything in your power to make the new hire feel welcome. Assign someone in their department to show them around the first day. Take them to lunch. If you can't personally do it, be sure to have someone else on the team take them. Assign someone as their "buddy" to help show them the ropes and monitor how things are progressing.

Remember, the reason you hired someone is that you needed a change. Now set up the conditions to implement that and to make them wildly successful. This takes active management. If you wait, it takes even more work. Never expect things to magically get better. The better you onboard and acclimate someone, the faster they will deliver impact and the faster you will all earn the results you are striving to achieve.

All the best,

Maynard

2

Financing Your Company

WHEN NOBODY WANTS TO GIVE YOU MONEY

GUEST LETTER BY JEREMY SCHNEIDER, MANAGING DIRECTOR AT THE WEBB INVESTMENT NETWORK.

Dear Founder,

While it can be disheartening (and frustrating) to feel like you're not making progress with fundraising, you should know that many WIN companies have been in a similar position at some point. Fundraising takes a lot of time and can be very distracting. It also can feel like you are starring in *Don Quixote,* chasing down windmills.

Our industry is quite extreme in that sometimes everyone wants to give you money, and other times, no one wants to invest in your company. If you're in the latter category, it's crucial to focus on the business to make the investment as attractive as possible. How you respond to these setbacks, and how you prioritize your time and effort, will have a big impact on your happiness and on your fundraising success.

- **First and foremost, are you speaking with the right people?** I cannot stress enough how important it is to be targeted and measured as you build your investor list. Have you had a chance to speak with investors and advisers who know the market well, who can give you advice, and who might be able to open doors for you? If you find yourself meeting with seemingly random investors at the early stage, there is a high likelihood that you might be barking up the wrong tree.
    - We often counsel our founders to categorize investors in different buckets (we call them "sorties"). Try to group three to five investors in each sortie, and reach out to each group individually rather than blasting everyone at once.

This approach may seem slower, but it often enables you to incorporate feedback and to build momentum as you move to each successive sortie.

- **Fundraising is all about building and maintaining momentum.** Once the lead falls into place, rounds normally come together very quickly. How does one find a lead? In your initial investor sortie, speak with a handful of leads and also individual angel investors who can commit before a lead is in place. Ultimately the lead will determine how a round comes together, but sometimes progress with great angels can also encourage a lead to move or introduce you to others they frequently work with. While it might feel counterintuitive, starting with some of the smaller players can sometimes yield a better overall outcome.
- **Are you setting yourself up for success?** Do you have any leverage going into these meetings? Often, the most important source of leverage for a founder going into fundraising is having plenty of runway (you do not need to raise, but feel the time is right). Does your "ask" for investors make sense? Are you raising an appropriate amount for the stage of your business? Do you have the right team and the right approach to tackle your market? Investors can latch on to perceived "deal killers." Perceived shortcomings can blind them to other virtues of the company, so buttoning up many major concerns in advance of meeting can make a big difference.
- **Are you internalizing and acting on the feedback from investors after a meeting?** If you start to detect a pattern in how investors respond (e.g., they think the idea is too early, they have questions about market, they have questions about competitors, etc.), it's important that you address these concerns and take this feedback to heart. It is easy to dismiss investor feedback (e.g., "Investor X only spent thirty minutes

with me, how could they possibly even understand the product I am building?"), but investors see many companies and have a good pulse on the market and when a company feels "fundable." If you have the luxury of being able to do this, sometimes pausing fundraising for a month or two to focus on the business and messaging can make a world of difference.

- **Are you being honest with yourself about momentum?** Momentum is palpable, and you know when you have it. Follow-up meetings do not necessarily mean momentum. Does the investor seem to be leaning in? Is he or she proactively reaching out to you with next steps, or do you find yourself constantly chasing people down? At WIN, we often compare the process of making an investment to falling in love. An investor who is excited about your company will jump through hoops to make things happen, and you will feel like you are being fast-tracked.
- **Start to think about Plan Bs.** Can you raise a smaller amount of money to make material progress? Are there other potential investors (e.g., corporate venture groups or industry players) who could add tremendous value and who might have more flexibility in their fund mandates? You should also have an idea of companies that could acquire your business and start reaching out to those contacts, if only to help build momentum as you engage with investors.

Some things to avoid:

- **It is easy to become bitter with the fundraising process.** Don't focus on other companies that seem to have an easy go of fundraising. Try not to disparage people who don't "get" what you're building. Investors are well-tuned to pick up these emotions, and often view them as a sign of weakness and lack of fortitude.

- **Avoid artificial deadlines or time pressures.** Investors know when something is moving, and when it is not. A rush for a follow-up meeting, needing clarity as the round is coming together, etc., often present investors with an excuse to pass. (You'll hear: "We cannot meet your deadline at this time.")
- **Do not be coy, or give runaround answers, to questions about the state of the business or fundraising to date.** Investors should do their homework, and they will eventually find the truth so it's much better to control this process and this dialogue, rather than try to hand-wave these questions away (again, this can give investors a reason to send a quick "pass" note). It's much, much better for an investor to give you money knowing the thorny challenges you're facing, rather than to give you money on somewhat false pretenses.

The fundraising process can make you a better CEO. Fundraising is a lot like sales, only this time you're not selling a product but rather shares in your company. Though the process may be grueling, it can offer an important window of self-reflection and a chance to tighten your story and focus on the important drivers of your business. Also, this experience can serve to encourage you and your team to make the next round of financing as compelling as possible. Talk to a few potential lead candidates for the next round and ask what they like to see in companies like yours. Be ruthlessly focused on getting to those figures (ideally six-plus months before you're out of cash), and the fundraising experience may be very different the next time around.

Best,

Jeremy

WHEN EVERYONE WANTS TO INVEST

GUEST LETTER BY JEREMY SCHNEIDER, MANAGING DIRECTOR AT THE WEBB INVESTMENT NETWORK

Dear Founder,

Take a moment to celebrate the rarefied air you are breathing right now. Many CEOs dream of being in this position, and you should feel great about capturing the attention and interest of so many investors. Below are a few pieces of advice that we've shared with our founders over the years. In general, these suggestions tie to a common theme: the importance of maintaining a long-term outlook in a high-pressure situation.

Breathe, and remember that it is just the very beginning of the journey.

It's easy to get caught up in the excitement and fervor of the fundraise. As someone who sits on the investor side of the table, I can only imagine how it must feel to be in your shoes.

Remember that *you* have the power to drive the process, timeline, and expectations. Investors can sometimes create an environment of pressure and deadlines, monopolizing your time and your imagination. Take stock of the situation, and ensure that you're talking to the right folks. Is there someone on your list that you've heard great things about, but with whom you have not yet made contact? If so, try to reach out and connect before the round is done. You will be working with your investors for a long time, and getting the right people involved will have a lasting impact on your business.

Keep counsel with friends and advisers.

Walk through and explain all of the varied points of different term sheets and different partner experiences with someone you trust. Just the act of putting your thoughts together, and of making a rational argument around why you should go with one offer or another (even a simple pros/cons list), can be of value. We recommend finding a neutral sounding board—whether that be a fellow founder or an early angel investor/adviser—to go through these exercises with you.

It is difficult to undo a commitment.

Try to resist the urge to continue raising smaller checks while you piece together the lead. Early commitments from friends and angels can add up quickly. Every $50K to $100K check counts, and the larger this pledged pool becomes, the harder it is to set expectations with your potential leads, and potentially to reset expectations with your committed angels if there is not enough space. Rather than confirming all the investment amounts at the beginning, you can communicate your appreciation and desire to work with someone without promising allocation or a specific dollar amount. Preserving flexibility at the start of the raise often pays off later in the process, and can prevent "broken glass" with friends and early supporters of the company.

Examine your biases.

Sometimes we encounter founders who are concerned about board dynamics, or who are worried about any potential challenge to company control. Others are very worried about dilution, to the point where they press their advantage too early. It's much easier to say than to do, but try to think through what set of choices will have the biggest long-term impact on your company. Sometimes finding a strong board member who believes in your team and vision, but who can also challenge you, is critical. Sometimes, a little more dilution early on can result in better outcomes for all. When you decide to move forward with a term sheet, it's important that you fully understand the reasons (and potential biases) behind your thinking, and to make a good choice for the long term.

Don't get ahead of your skis when it comes to valuation.

We've seen this movie many times. A company is performing well and is "hot," and the founder is able to raise ahead of their metrics—at a lofty valuation—from a firm eager to win the round and secure allocation. Silicon Valley press has a tendency to celebrate pre-money valuations without fully understanding the double-edged sword they present. These rounds, while they might make you feel like you are building tremendous value, often present meaningful difficulties down the road. If your company's growth falters or does not meet expectations, you'll run the risk of having to answer to an angry and disappointed group of investors. If the macroclimate changes, or if your company, for whatever reason, momentarily loses its luster, you could face the prospect of a down round, which can have lasting effects on company and investor morale. This is not to say that you should purposefully sandbag your valuation for fear of not living up to expectations. Rather, it's to suggest that you choose a number, which feels fair, which you believe you and your team can live up to, and which you believe creates a foundation for a win-win outcome.

In the battle for allocation, remember that you can cast the deciding vote.

There is always flexibility on all sides of a negotiation. Many investors have gone through this process hundreds of times, whereas founders go through it a handful of times at most. If you are in a competitive situation, recognize that you have more power than you might think. If it is important for you to preserve space for pro rata or for strategic new investors, make this clear in the negotiation and set aside some allocation. Great partners rarely push back on this, as they also see the value in having more helpful hands around the table. If it's important for you that the option pool look a certain way, make this case early in the process with your lead.

Be upfront, decisive, and understanding throughout the process.

Remember that this is a long game, and that many of the people you encounter in this process are folks that you will cross paths with again. Treat them in such a way that the next time you meet, they are as eager to work with you as they are right now. You may not always be in this enviable fundraising position, and it's important to establish good relationships with the investor community and not to burn any bridges (in particular, false expectations around timing or valuations can cause future friction).

Finally, understand the tactics that investors may employ.

Investors have a number of tools that they may use to win the deal or to exert influence. Some of the most frequent to be aware of include:

- **Exploding term sheets.** Investors will rush to provide you with a term sheet before others do, and they will sometimes include a clause that makes the term sheet expire if you do not accept it within a few days. A good way to counteract this maneuver is to say that you want to do more diligence on the firm (this can give you time), and that you are looking for a great partner and thus do not understand why there is a need to emphasize a short time horizon. If they are trying to make a case that they will be tremendous partners, then this is not a great way to start the relationship.
- **Guilt.** Investors may try to make you feel bad if you do not choose to work with them. As a founder, it's important to separate your own personal feelings from what is best for the business. Simply be polite and let them know that while you

are so appreciative of their interest to work with your team, you still need to evaluate your options carefully to choose what is best for the future of your company.

- **Fancy outings and exclusive gatherings.** You may be invited to unique events and experiences. Understand that there is an investor agenda at play, and use the time with the investor to see how they behave socially and with other founders and peers.

Congratulations again on being in this enviable position, and try to appreciate how rare it is to captivate the minds of so many investors. Also remember that this is the just the start of the race, and that the truly difficult parts of building your company lie ahead. It often takes years for companies to reach their destiny, so my advice is to not rush this fundraise. Be as thoughtful about this process as you have been about assembling your team and building your product.

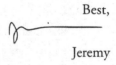

Best,

Jeremy

WHEN YOU ARE SETTING TERMS FOR YOUR SEED ROUND

GUEST LETTER BY JONATHAN PINES, DIRECTOR AT THE WEBB INVESTMENT NETWORK.

Dear Founder,

First of all, congrats! If someone wants to invest in your business, then you are already off to a great start. Now you just need to agree on the details, structure your round, and start a positive relationship with your investor group. Here are a few things to keep in mind as you go through this process.

Do your research.

- **Read up on round structure.** Many early stage rounds are done with convertible notes or simple agreements for future equity (SAFEs). Since SAFEs are agreements for *future* equity, the terms end up being dependent on terms set at the time of the SAFE and at the time of the future equity fundraise. It is therefore important to understand how these contracts work, and to understand common terms like cap, discount, pro rata, liquidation preference, and MFN (most favored nation).
- **Do the math and create a model!** Convertible note math is tricky, and the results are not intuitive. Build a simple spreadsheet to understand how conversion will work, and include all rounds through your Series A. Calculate your dilution, and look at how the share price changes from round to round.

Check your assumptions.

- **What is your next round?** Your next stage might be a Series A, another early stage round, or profitability. Many companies raise more than one early stage round, so experiment with this—especially if you are raising a smaller seed round. Also ask around to estimate the size and price of your Series A (as a rule of thumb, the size will be 20–30% of the post-money valuation). Get a few data points, and don't expect an outlier.
- **What are your milestones?** Talk to some founders and investors, and try to get a sense for what it will take to get to that next stage. It might be a certain amount of revenue, product usage, team size, or something else. Your milestones should be both realistic and sufficient: You don't want to run out of money before hitting them, nor do you want to get there only to find out that you set your targets too low to raise the next round.
- **How much money do you need?** How much time, which team members, and what kinds of resources will you need to hit your milestones—and how much money will that take? Be conservative and leave some breathing room. Things usually go slower than expected, and raising the next round will take time, too. We usually advise our companies to aim for at least eighteen months of runway in a seed round. If this is not possible, focus on your milestones and add some extra buffer.

Choose a fair price.

- **Consider your dilution.** Many seed rounds bear 20–25% dilution, meaning the seed investors will own that much of your company before the next round. Sometimes this can be as low as 15% or as high as 30%, and in unusual cases outside this range, too. There are no hard rules here, but this can provide one data point on where to start.

- **Leave room for upside.** Your first investors are taking a risk and supporting you early, at a stage where most companies will fail. Treat them well, and set them up for success with a price increase in the next round. If you are already close to your milestones, then a small step up might make sense. If you are just getting started and hoping for $2M revenue in eighteen months, then a bigger valuation jump is in order. Check your model and discuss what is fair.
- **Market pricing trumps all.** Ultimately, the terms are set between you and your investors, and anything goes as long as you agree with them. If you have a lot of interest you can be choosy, and if not, you may need to take whatever you can get. Either way, try to stay within a reasonable range. You don't want to give up too much of your company, and you also don't want your investors to get a raw deal by paying the same price as the next round (or to have a price decrease, which can cause other issues).
- **Work together to set terms.** If you don't already have significant commitments to invest in your company, keep an open mind. If you try to set terms upfront on your own (or with someone who is writing a tiny check), you may create mismatched expectations. Work with your early champions to set terms that make sense for everyone, and set the tone for collaboration.

Think about the long term.

- **Choose your partners carefully.** Good investors will be great partners for you in the future, and they will help you grow your company and raise future financing. Ask around about their reputation and their ability to help.

- **Prioritize what matters most to you.** Some founders want mostly financial support, and others are focused on getting help and a good network from their investors. Some want to minimize dilution, and others want extra runway. Rank your priorities, and then don't sweat the small details. If you are pressing your advantage on one axis (e.g., price), be mindful of any trade-offs you may be creating.
- **It's not a competition.** If you have a friend raising money at high terms, or if you are reading articles about hot companies, it can be tempting to constantly compare yourself to them. Focus on your business. A year from now the comparison will not matter, and having the right amount of capital and support will be crucial!

Best,

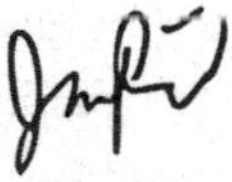

Jonathan

WHEN YOU NEED TO SET A VALUATION

Dear Founder,

Setting valuation for a startup is kind of like trying to figure out odds on the Super Bowl before the game is played. It's challenging, but here, the winners and losers don't go home after the game is over, the bet is settled, and the nachos are gone. Investors and entrepreneurs will be working together for years—and years, and years.

Of course you want the maximum valuation for your company, but it's important to take a long-term perspective. It might seem like you won if the deal is overpriced and you gave up less of your company, but in reality that comes with the price of an investor with a board seat who is steaming about overpaying for an overvalued deal.

We once met founders of a company who had raised on slightly aggressive terms, in part because of how aggressive their financial projections were. When they failed to meet expectations, they had thought it would be okay, as their projections were "pitch deck metrics," which everyone knows to discount. Their new board member was less forgiving, and now believed that he had overpaid for the investment—not a good dynamic in the boardroom.

Companies need to set a valuation to determine what the company is worth and what percentage of shares go to new investors versus stay with the company. Generally speaking, I find that entrepreneurs overly emphasize valuation because it comes with prestige and because every incremental bit of dilution given up seems like a massive loss when the entrepreneur truly believes their company will be a huge success. On the flip side, investors can often be overly aggressive on terms, choosing to optimize for hitting a certain ownership threshold over ensuring that the company is well-positioned to grow two to three times by the time they next need to raise.

It's a delicate dance, but the thing to keep in mind is that everyone must work together to make the company as successful as it can be. Some things to think about:

When do you raise money? Timing matters. Raising money with more progress is better as long as you have enough cash. It's always better to raise in a position of strength, not weakness. People see when you are desperate. Raising money is like accessing credit—really easy to get when you don't need it and really difficult when you do. Also, remember, there are a lot of things beyond your control. In early to mid-2008 companies saw good valuations, but months later the world melted and they would not have been able to get the same valuation—if they could have raised money at all.

How much do you raise? Well, how much money do you need? In some ways, startups need less money today than they used to, but you need to raise enough so that you are not constantly raising money. We recommend modeling eighteen to twenty-four months of runway (the longer the runway, the better, as things will usually take longer than you expect).

What valuation is the market willing to give you? You have to determine what the company—your idea and team—is really worth. Solicit a couple of friendly sources for their feedback on what the market is currently paying to invest in a company like yours. This answer can vary with time, based on your revenue, your sector, or recent news about you or competitors. We worked with one startup that was able to raise easily up to their Series B—until Google entered their market and offered their services for free. And trends change—in 2013, you could raise a round easily with a deck that started with "Uber for X," where X could be laundry, alcohol, even furniture. Try that today, and you might not get VCs to respond to emails.

Leverage between VCs and founders will also change based on the investment climate. When there's abundant venture capital at play, expect to be able to raise more and give up less as investors clamor over fewer deals. Weirdly, you may end up in a scenario where you need to negotiate against yourself—if VCs compete against one another too hard on terms, they may end up paying based on your anticipated value in six, twelve, or even eighteen months. Should you ultimately miss these projections, will you be able to raise your next round or sell at a step-up? And if you can't, what actions might that investor take? (Hint: They aren't good.)

With all of this in mind, companies can start thinking about dilution. Typically, we see companies give away somewhere between 15% and 25% of their company for most rounds of funding, with smaller percentages as companies get later stage and have more options. Try to give away enough to be worth great investors' time and attention, but not so much that you lose control of the business long term.

Lastly, valuation is not the only term that matters. One time I saw a term sheet from an investor that demanded three different board seats—for a seed round. I coached the founder to back away as fast as humanly possible. Term sheets can include provisions about number of board seats, observer seats, rules for handling debt, how a CEO can be dismissed, and more. Ask your friends for horror stories, and always ask a lawyer to read your docs before signing (and read them yourself, too). Conversely, you may *want* to take a lower valuation, provided that it results in the best possible board member for your business.

In general, we coach our founders to optimize for people first. You'll be with your investors a long time, and what valuation you got in what round will almost never matter as much as how much integrity you had at all stages. Don't give away excessive amounts, but if you can think abundantly and focus on making the pie bigger for everyone, I promise you this process will be easier and more pleasant. Some of my team members at WIN put it this way: "In eighteen months, you want your new investors to look smart—just not *too* smart." That's the real secret to the best deal—and biggest return—for everyone.

All the best,

Maynard

WHEN YOU'VE JUST RAISED YOUR FIRST ROUND OF FUNDING

GUEST LETTER BY KEVIN WEBB, DIRECTOR AT THE WEBB INVESTMENT NETWORK

Dear Founder,

Congratulations! First things first, some amount of (reasonable) celebration is in order. You and a couple friends—maybe with a product, maybe not—have just been valued by professional investors to be worth a large amount of money. So, drink some (reasonable) champagne, go for a hike, invite your investors to laser tag. Raising outside money is hopefully the first of many milestones, and it's worth pausing to mark the occasion.

But then, of course, the real work starts. Assuming you've raised enough to give you 18 to 24 months' runway, you have approximately 75 to 100 weeks from now until you need to already have more cash in the bank. To put yourself in the best position for your next round, you'll want to be done with your raise with 2 to 3 months of cash left in the bank, which means starting the raise another 2 to 3 months before that.

In other words, you basically have 12 to 18 months (50 to 75 weeks) to build a compelling business. During that time, you'll want to get the most out of your shiny new investors. Here are some ideas for doing so.

Write updates.

Short and frequent communication is better than long and sporadic missives. Make updates easy to produce. With so many things happening constantly within your business, writing updates can serve as a chance to reflect on your top-line goals—and a way to stay honest about your business's direction.

Updates also, importantly, can incentivize your investors into helping you. At the risk of generalizing, we're a competitive bunch, so recognizing the help of an investor can inspire others into helping you. So, every time you send an update, include asks, and call out the people who went above and beyond to contribute. Recognition in these updates will motivate the rest of your investors to want to help that much more.

As you get into the rhythm of sharing updates, you can ask investors what metrics or figures they think are worth tracking as you progress to your next round. Adding these numbers into weekly or monthly updates will only push you to start automating collection and presentation of these data, setting you up better for the long run.

Seek intros.

One of the primary ways any early investor works is through facilitating introductions. These come in many flavors: customer discovery, potential hires, potential customers, professional services, other investors, etc. As you're in the driver's seat, it's important to chase introductions that are actually needle-moving for you.

Assume with most introductions that you only get one chance to impress someone—it's not a bad idea to ask investors if they believe the timing is right to approach a given contact.

Build an informal board.

We've seen founders put together an informal board, either as a quasi board of directors, or as an advisory board of potential customers.

An informal board gets you all the advantages of a traditional board, but without the potential risks and formal governance of a real board (i.e., they can't ever fire you). Choose people you like and who can add value, and ask them to meet regularly every month or quarter. Ask that they hold you accountable. This structure can give you valuable experience going into your next round, and it can potentially surface and kill off issues that—without their pattern recognition—could lead you astray.

Best of all, if it doesn't help, you can wind it down whenever you want!

An advisory board is a bit different; it's a way to turn people you'd like to be customers into advisers. Done well, it's an elegant Jedi trick—you transform someone who might be put off as a customer into someone who will actively counsel you on how to make them want to give you money. You can meet these people ad hoc, or get them together regularly for broader feedback. Remember: even incredibly accomplished people like to feel recognized for their time and insights. Give credit freely, and they'll be excited to help. Some might even be hires down the road.

A note of caution: Before you have some evidence of product/market fit, these boards can prove to be far more of a distraction than they are valuable. We've seen "advisory boards" comprised of people with little experience relevant to the company. That's a mistake; view these advisory slots as a scarce resource, only given to people with immense expertise. You may also want to plan for obsolescence; often, advisers aren't relevant for more than approximately six months of a business's life. Structure agreements accordingly.

Get management help.

We see many first-time founders. In this role, you can expect a huge range of new, stressful, or time-consuming tasks that are completely unrelated to what's most important (building a long-term, defensible business). While investors should never be able to know more than you about the special sauce of your business, they may know much more about distractions that can derail you. They can help on a wide range of interpersonal issues that constantly spring up.

Seek honest counsel on your next round.

Now that your seed money is in the bank, start thinking about what incredible story you can tell by the time you need to raise your next round of financing. The more proverbial boxes you can check, the better leverage you'll have in fundraising. Although raising a great next round shouldn't be your only goal, it does have a strong correlation with future success; by definition, great Series A lead investors earn their reputations by picking the best Series A companies.

Ask about the failures.

Every investor who's been around long enough has seen businesses flame out. Ask about these situations—they are informative lessons, and often make for good stories.

Avoid headaches.

Investors can be tremendously helpful, but they can also be tremendous distractions. After meetings, honestly assess what you got out of your time with them—in terms of resources provided, energy given or taken, etc. Maynard often wonders how much he would pay for advice a particular board member provides in meetings. Sometimes, the people most eager to take your time have the least to offer.

Consider their input. Make up your own mind.

Again, no one runs your company but you. In general, investors' incentives are tied closely to yours. When they offer advice, you can typically assume good intentions and often there's hard-earned wisdom behind it, but ultimately, it's your role to consider their insights, weigh them against evidence and your own perspective, and make up your own mind. Investors bet on you to process information and to make the decisions you think are best.

Treat them like advocates.

Lastly, remember that early investors have relationships with other investors that will span years, if not decades. If they're seeing your story progress, they can—if you want—be warming up your future leads well before you need to think about raising more capital. Their reputations are also on the line, so the more they've seen, the more earnestly they can get other investors excited.

Naturally, we're happy to help on any of these. But first, go (reasonably) celebrate; week one doesn't start until you do.

Best,

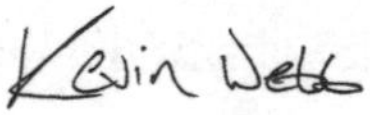

Kevin

WHEN YOU NEED TO THINK ABOUT COMPENSATION

Dear Founder,

Compensation is a complicated topic. It's filled with nuances that are very important to understand. Do your homework and be aware of the ramifications.

I believe that the best startups have teams that are scrappy and have incentives aligned across all shareholders. Founder compensation should be tied to performance. From an investor standpoint, we are providing the capital (and hopefully some help). If the company wins, we win. If the company fails, we lose. I personally prefer winning, so I like to see incentives that drive everyone toward success.

Often that means that founders are willing to share heavily in the risk. I have a visceral reaction to people who don't want to take any risk—especially when everyone involved is taking risks. As an investor, I'm always looking for entrepreneurs who are willing to take the same bet on themselves that I'm taking on them. That means getting a big equity stake but forgoing a big salary.

So, how much should founders pay themselves? It should be enough to take care of your basic needs so you can focus 100% on the company, but not as large a salary as you would make at an established company—that would drain too much cash. Worse, it reduces your leverage when you explain to new hires why their offers may be below market rate. Startups by nature are never flush with cash, and they must preserve the cash they have to invest in the company. Equity should be your primary fiscal motivation. Once the company is further along, CEOs can consider asking for a higher salary. For example, we often see salary bumps after the company has raised a Series B.

What about the rest of the team? I like to see everyone—employees included—taking a risk, but you want to pay them enough so they will be committed fully to the company, and not have to take another job or live off of savings. As the company grows you will likely come closer to paying market rates, but in the beginning this may not be possible. Offering everyone equity is a great way to get everyone aligned with what is good for employees and good for the enterprise. Consider employing a sliding scale, where employees can choose whether cash now, or equity, is more important. I tend to gravitate toward employees willing to take risks, but this may rule out talented people who have families, mortgages, etc.

Are there any exceptions? As always, you need to understand the full picture so you know when to break the rules. When Meg Whitman hired me, eBay was in a difficult position and she wanted me to fix it. While Gateway had compensated me generously, her offer had to be compelling enough to convince me to move my family to the Bay Area, and join a troubled startup. It's necessary to know what will "move" them to fully commit to you. A killer engineer will have several offers with both a great salary and great equity. Know what other startups are offering to remain competitive. (Do not compare yourself to bigger companies—you will be offering a lower cash package but giving them higher upside.) While it might sometimes be necessary to make exceptions, understand every compensation decision you make (or break) will set a precedent.

Mission matters. There are thousands of companies talented people could conceivably work for. You'll have far more leverage in negotiation if what you're working on, and how you communicate that mission, appeals viscerally to someone's sense of purpose. And, assuming you properly grow and invest in that person, their retention is likely to be far longer than more money-motivated peers.

What else to consider? How you are compensated matters, and how you treat others matters. There are many founder CEOs who don't take any salary or any additional stock, as they know the best return for them is to grow the impact of the stake they have. This is rare, though. In the beginning, stock awards should be solely based on time vesting. As you mature, sometimes performance hurdles are added on top of the time vesting, and by the time you become public you are almost always required to have 50/50 performance-based and time-based stock.

Having spent time with many entrepreneurs, I know that financial gain is not what's most important to the best entrepreneurs we meet. If you are like them, you want to change the world. Money is a secondary objective. You are willing to trade a big salary, security, and 99.9% of your time because you can't imagine doing anything else.

All the best,

Maynard

WHEN YOU NEED TO SET A BUDGET

Dear Founder,

In the very early days, you can probably manage expenses pretty easily.

However, I still advocate having a simple plan for expenses—know what you are allocating toward head count, marketing, software, computers, lease, furniture, etc. Even in the early days, you can track how you are doing against what you thought you were going to spend, and most importantly, if there is a delta, you can find out why.

Once you are growing—and certainly when you are between a Series A and Series B round of funding—you will likely need a more formal budget process. This is a blend of art and science.

The art of implementing a budget process is to ensure:

1. You are fully (or near fully) funding the most important things.
2. It is clear where the money is being spent.
3. There are mechanisms in place to spend wisely.

It's common for big companies to spend many months on the budget process. They often set top-down targets and ask for bottom-up requests. The problem is, these two camps generally don't reconcile, creating tension and leading to budget wars. Until things get settled, people often feel like winners and losers.

When I was at IBM, the head of finance in my location tried to gamify this tension. He had several personas that he had developed for characters in the budget process. One was "The Gardener," whom he told us to be careful of—every time you cut a branch, new shoots appear. His solution? "Cut it off at the root." Another character was, "The Dying Man," someone who was clearly convinced that the organization could not keep its head above water. In this case his solution was, "Throw him a lifeline."

But startups don't have time for this kind of overhead or distraction. My recommendations:

- **While setting an annual plan is good, understand that your business is probably too early in its life cycle to have this cast in concrete.** Revenue projections are always wrong in some fashion. Therefore, plan to true up the budget and the actual spend every quarter. This way you can see and tend to what your growing business needs. If sales aren't ramping, maybe hiring slows. Conversely, if growth is exploding, maybe you free up more spend.
- **Instill financial discipline early.** Spend money like it is your own. (And if you're not great with money, spend it like your very frugal family member.)
- **Get alignment between the executive team and the board on the overarching goals.** This means: revenue, gross margin, profit/loss, head count, etc.
- **Work on allocation.** I've always found it wise to reserve some allocation at the CEO level. This enables you to have resources for unforeseen issues as opposed to clawing things back from somebody. (It's better to never give something than to give and then take away.) At WIN, I have 10% of the budget allocated as "discretionary," so if we make a mistake and don't have enough funding for something, I can decide to still do it and relieve some of the pressure.
- **Create a challenge.** If you are close to what you want to spend (over by only 5–10%), put that in as a challenge that the whole team is committed to solve. Most companies wind up hiring more slowly than planned and also underestimate the attrition, which will likely cover your challenge issues. Remember this truth: People spend lots of time arguing for

specific, exact head-count numbers even though they are generally not going to hit them.

- **There is no entitlement.** Just because you received a big allocation last year doesn't mean that is the starting point this year. At eBay, we asked everyone to shave 5% efficiency off their base each year, which we called "save to invest."

With budgeting, perhaps the most important rule is this: Always look to get better and spend smarter. Those extra dollars saved can be allocated to do more strategic things.

All the best,

Maynard

WHEN YOU NEED TO SPEND YOUR MONEY WISELY

Dear Founder,

You should always spend your money like it's your own. In this letter, I offer tips on how to spend money appropriately, including examples of where we see founders misspend. After that, I share what to do if you're running into money challenges and need to course correct.

Entrepreneurs are typically so focused on preserving enough cash to stay alive that I don't usually find them blowing money. It's rare to see fat expense accounts or even market rate salaries (and when I see those things at startups, I typically run for the hills). While spending too much isn't the problem, spending on the wrong things at the wrong time often is. These are some of the things founders miscalculate:

Spending too much too early. If you don't have a product yet, don't spend much on anything other than developing the product.

Not spending enough. When the flywheel is really going, it might be necessary to spend money on increasing sales and marketing to grow even faster. In other instances, it becomes essential to spend more building the architecture and systems to stay ahead of the growth. (This is the scenario that led to me joining eBay as President of Technology in 1999 to keep the site up and running through rapid growth.)

Hiring a sales team too early. If you are building an enterprise product, having a big sales organization before you have a product is a mistake. Salesforce is a great example of a company that did not invest in sales until it was necessary. Instead, it invested its resources in developing a useful product. And the founders and early employees pitched the service wherever they went—including while waiting in line at the supermarket.

Beefing up on administrative matters in the beginning. Building finance or HR teams too early is not prudent. Initially, those can—and probably should—be outsourced.

Falling for office space. While most entrepreneurs are inherently frugal, many have a blind spot for nice office facilities. The justifications for a hip, well-located space can be tempting—this space will attract employees, and it will impress clients and press. Yet, often the cost simply isn't worth it, and worse, getting a space that says, "We made it!," when really, you haven't, can draw the wrong talent and infuse your culture with a sense of false accomplishment.

Paying full salaries. Offering high salaries at an early stage is a recipe for burning cash. At a startup, everyone should be taking risk, and compensation should be a combination of salary and equity. If the business is successful, the equity will be far more valuable than cash.

Underutilizing all of the available resources. If you need help, ask for it from your advisers and board. Don't think of your board members as just folks who tell you what to do; put them to work. The best entrepreneurs know how to leverage their network and are not shy about asking for advice and introductions.

Wasting time. Capital is not only money; time is just as valuable, and managing it well is just as crucial. You have to do as much as you can every day, week, month, and year. Utilizing time effectively is one of the most important skills in an entrepreneur's arsenal.

Okay, so those are all the cardinal rules of what not to do, and as a result, how to spend money wisely, but what about when you've already had a misstep? You should always know how much cash you are burning each month and how much time you have left to live. As the CEO, it's your job to move far and fast enough to raise more funding when you need it—and at advantageous terms.

If you are not getting the traction you had expected for whatever reason (e.g., maybe the product isn't ready, the market is not quite there, or sales aren't being executed), you have to figure out how to change the burn rate to extend your life.

While you can feel horrible about having to do this, this is the cold reality of managing your company. Just like in the rest of your financial life, if you are not able to pay your bills, you'll have to find a way to spend less or earn more.

Let's look at some specific ways to get costs in line with where the business expectations now are.

If you have more office space than you need: Explore how you can either get out of the lease or sublease the space.

If you can't afford to hire people: Slow down! Put a freeze on hiring. If the product is not ready, you don't need salespeople—or a lot of the other hires you'll need later, but probably can do without at the moment.

If you've already hired too many people: As painful as it is, if you've added a bunch of people too quickly, you'll have to let the nonessential hires go and keep the folks around who can get you to the promised land. You have to be very cautious about this. Laying someone off is one the nastiest things an employer ever has to do. It's far worse than having to fire someone for cause. If nothing else, this will prove to you the importance of managing your money right from the beginning

If you are spending too much on payroll: Obviously you will have to tweak your own compensation. Sometimes people are willing to take voluntary pay cuts. However, you must be aware that once you start to either reduce or defer salaries, it's a signal that the business is in trouble and people will start to look for other jobs.

Effectively managing money for a company is a never-ending process. Even public companies have trouble doing this well, as evidenced by layoffs. There are times when you need to be frugal and times when you need to fuel growth and capture the market opportunity. Developing the judgment to know which actions to take at which time is where the magic happens!

All the best,

Maynard

WHEN YOU NEED TO FIGURE OUT COMPENSATION FOR YOUR SALES TEAM

GUEST LETTER BY PETE CITTADINI, EXPERIENCED STARTUP CEO

Dear Founder,

Sales compensation is one of the most important things to figure out. It's also pretty simple to mess up, which can lead to dire consequences.

When I was prepping for the CEO position at a growing company, I met with the VP of sales for a glass of wine at Madera, in the famous five-star Rosewood Sand Hill Hotel in Menlo Park.

"Well, let's talk about quota and comp," I suggested.

We all know this is a very important part of running a business, but I wasn't expecting anything unusual. Then, he told me quota was $800,000. I thought that was really, *really* low.

"How much do you pay?" I asked

"Three hundred thousand dollars on average per sales rep," he replied.

Whoa, that seemed out of balance. In my experience it could be as low as $200,000 and maybe, in exceptional cases, as high as $275,000–$280,000. Yet here, everyone was treated at the high end. That's crazy at a startup where cash is king. Then he told me they paid the reps before the cash was collected.

I wanted to jump out of my seat! Not only was the quota too low and the comp too high, but the reps were paid on the bookings, not the cash coming in. That was completely incorrect—you can only pay when cash comes in so you have something to offset commissions.

That year at the end of their Q1, the company paid $560,000 in cash to the sales organization for bringing in an IOU of $900,000 (cashless bookings for the quarter). They were thrilled. "Has this ever happened to you anywhere else?" I asked. "Why should it happen here?"

The reps were laughing all the way to the bank and the company was left in a vulnerable position. This was an issue of gross negligence, and it was an absolute mess. I was in the fetal position for the first week after joining, wondering: *What the hell did I get myself into?*

Yet the amazing part is that with just some basic "101" work, we were able to improve the company tenfold in a short period time. It didn't even require doing anything sophisticated. Everyone hates the basics. They think basics are beneath them and basics aren't for people of superior intellect. Not true! Look at the results of the NFL team, the New England Patriots, led by the duo of Bill Belichick and Tom Brady. They are constantly focused on the basics and sticking to the game plan.

Everything that was required was already there—the founders were awesome, the product and market fit was awesome, and the board was top-shelf. We just had to work on the basics; we had to address the easy stuff. Here's what we did:

Set the right quotas and comp structure. We made three levels that were based on experience:

$1.2 million sales quota, $240,000 total compensation in salary and bonus

$1.4 million sales quota, $260,000 total compensation in salary and bonus

$1.6 million sales quota, $280,000 total compensation in salary and bonus

Add incentives. We have simple plans that also pay well in accelerators. The plan begins paying at 6%, then moves to 12%, then moves to 18%. That's a highly motivating plan. This way, superstars get paid well. One individual is already at 35% of quota by the end of January—I think motivated by our plan.

Make sure all deals come in cash upfront. Cash must come in before compensation is paid. Commissions must be based on cash collected—not just securing a contract.

Have the right number of sales reps. You need sales reps, but you need not go overboard with hiring a lot of reps early. We had thirty reps when I joined and I brought that down to seventeen people because many of them had the wrong mentality. A lot of people left on their own. One quit on my first day! Others had to be fired. One of the board members resigned. I don't think I'm the most hated person at the company today, but for the first six months I was. That's okay; we needed the right people with the right management team. Now we have over fifty people and we did all that within ten months.

Don't overpay people in cash. The big incentive should be there in equity. That's the brass ring.

Invest in your product. You want cash from VCs to go into the product—and investing in evolving and improving it. That's what's most important in the early days of a startup.

We are now experiencing great things. Soon we will bring in more cash than we spend on running the business. Change happened with emotional turbulence with the early cast of employees, but by changing the very simple business basics, we got exactly where we need to be.

You must be aware that spending money for growth at all costs is no longer in vogue. The definition of business is for it to make a profit and cash flows as you drive growth. You want to build something solid, solvent, and sustainable.

All the best,

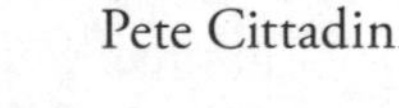

Pete Cittadini

WHEN YOU NEED TO UNDERSTAND WATERFALLS, LAYER CAKES, AND CAP TABLES (OR HOW TO PROTECT THE TRUE VALUE OF YOUR EQUITY)

GUEST LETTER BY HARSH PATEL, CO-FOUNDER AND MANAGING PARTNER OF WIREFRAME VENTURE AND WEBB INVESTMENT NETWORK AFFILIATE, AND JEREMY SCHNEIDER, MANAGING DIRECTOR AT THE WEBB INVESTMENT NETWORK

Dear Founder,

At a time when capital seems plentiful and late-stage valuations seem to be ever increasing, we thought it would be wise to share (or remind you of) some important lessons that directly affect your personal financial success.

Whenever we see huge M&A deals or IPOs, we instinctively assume that all those years of intense work by the founders were finally and rightfully paid off. However, the reality is that founder outcomes vary widely, including some cases where founders end up with surprisingly little from an otherwise great exit. The straightforward reason for this may simply be too much dilution along the way—having to raise too much capital relative to price by the time you're able to achieve an exit. While certainly difficult for founders, this scenario is typically not a surprise but rather something you're aware of and managing along the way. The more insidious scenario is driven by overly aggressive expectations and cap table complexity, which is our focus here.

One of the most important roles of a founder is to set and manage expectations of all constituents—employees, investors, partners, customers, and press. You paint the picture of what is possible someday, but also what should be expected at each step along the way. At any point in time, your startup's value will be determined by a unique combination of macro market conditions, quality of team and product, scarcity, business traction, and comparable company transactions. Know and use that information to generate your own "stretch-but-rational" valuation expectations for the next financing as well as the exit. In parallel, you're setting expectations for the performance you must deliver to justify that valuation.

It may seem perfectly rational to maximize valuation at each step, in exchange for accepting other deal terms that you deem unlikely to be triggered or of minimal negative impact (e.g., preferences, ratchets, warrants, debt). Far too often, though, numbers are missed and expectations are not met. Your company may still be performing well by any reasonable standard—yet "underperforming" relative to the expectations you embedded into your financing terms. If that happens, founders are often surprised at just how much personal value they may have lost. That's because founders and employees tend to think of their personal stake in terms of fully diluted ownership percentage (e.g.,"I own X% of the company."). So, if I own 10% of my company when it's valued at $100M but it later sells for $50M, at least I still get $5M right?! Well—not likely.

Actual cash returns to shareholders are determined using a liquidation waterfall analysis against your cap table. Imagine that your cap table is a layer cake. At the bottom of the cake, is common stock (typically founders and employees), and above that sits a new layer every time you raise financing—Series A preferred stock, above that Series B etc., and finally any debt is at the top. Each layer may also have its own set of terms (e.g., size, dividends, preferences, ratchets, etc.). When an exit happens, the proceeds are distributed one layer at a time—according to each layer's particular terms—from the top down. The effect is that each layer of the cake becomes "denser" as you move from the bottom (sponge cake) to the top (brownie). As long as your company meets or beats the expectations you built into your cap table, all layers should participate in the outcome as you'd expect. But if not, that cake starts to get squeezed from the top as your valuation is compressed. The larger the gap between expectations and reality, the more forceful this compression will be. When pressure is applied, the lowest/softest layers get squeezed more than the dense layers at the top. In a worst-case scenario, the brownie may be fine but the sponge cake (you) is flattened. This metaphor explains why your theoretical fully diluted ownership percentage of the total exit value may be far different than your actual payout.

A FEW SUGGESTIONS

- Don't apologize or feel guilty for considering your own financial outcome. Both founders and investors are rightfully focused on the dream and building a long-term successful company, but your investors have a portfolio and you don't. If they can model their return profile and internal rate of return (IRR), so can you.
- If you're not doing so already, consider using an online tool to manage your cap table. Services like Carta, Solium, Capyx, and others can streamline your cap table management and most also offer exit scenario modeling with liquidation waterfalls. Familiarize yourself with how such an analysis works.
- Before each financing, reevaluate your exit scenarios and take them into account when you consider what amount and terms you're seeking. If you raise at a high valuation driven by very aggressive expectations, you're essentially pinning your outcome to the most aggressive scenario. Any failure to meet that plan will come at your own expense.
- Like entropy, cap table complexity only increases. Try to avoid—or at least delay—allowing complex financial terms into your cap table. Recognize that a "good deal" should consider all terms, not just valuation.

We encourage founders to fully understand what you are signing up for when you raise money, and how cap table complexity compounds over time. You can be visionary and focused on the long term while still setting rational expectations along the way. None of this will matter if everything goes perfectly to plan. Yet since that rarely happens, plan for a range of scenarios and ensure you always protect the personal value of what you're building.

Best,

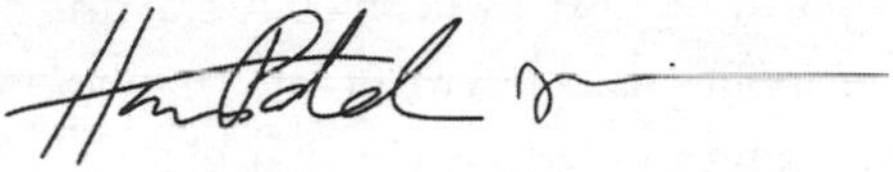

Harsh Patel and Jeremy Schneider

WHEN YOU WONDER IF PHILANTHROPY HAS A PLACE IN A STARTUP

Dear Founder,

If you're reading this letter, you must be wondering whether or not philanthropy has a place in a startup.

I have a very strong opinion about this: YES.

We've all been very blessed in our lives with talent and access to opportunity. Even when you're starting out, scrappy and small, caring about others less fortunate than you says a lot about the kind of company you are trying to build.

I've witnessed the wonders of doing so. As a part of eBay going public, Jeff Skoll and Pierre Omidyar created a foundation, which helped establish a strong culture of giving back. This inspired me personally, and it led me to create our own family foundation after I was fortunate enough to have provided for my family.

Salesforce was also inspired by the eBay Foundation and looked to the eBay model when it started its own initiative in 1999. Marc Benioff built on this idea and extended it. From day one, he implemented a 1-1-1 model, dedicating 1% of equity, 1% of employee time, and 1% of product to nonprofits and educational institutions. Through www.salesforce.org, Salesforce technology has powered more than 32,000 nonprofit and education institutions; Salesforce and its philanthropic entities have provided more than $168 million in grants; and Salesforce employees have logged more than 2.3 million volunteer hours to improve communities around the world.

When I was recruited to be the CEO of LiveOps, I insisted that implementing the 1-1-1 model was one of the criteria for me taking the job. We had an internal team of volunteers manage the program's creation and ongoing effort. Our employees felt proud of this work and most candidates coming through the recruiting process remarked on how it differentiated our company.

Now, I know what you might be thinking:

- *I don't have enough equity to give away 1%—and I don't know if it will even be worth anything.*
- *I'm trying to manage cash burn tightly, so I don't have cash to give.*
- *I expect big things out of my team and they are working like crazy; how can I ask them to spend more time on this?*

The good news? This is all way easier than it sounds or looks. Case in point: Salesforce Ventures, the company's investment arm, encourages its portfolio companies to make giving back part of their business model from the start, and dozens of their portfolio companies, including Appirio, Box, DocuSign, Demandbase, and InsideSales have adopted the 1-1-1 model through the Pledge 1% initiative.

So what should you do to get going?

- **Start gently.** Participate in a charity drive around the holidays to collect food, toys, etc. Celebrate how much you have raised or given.
- **Let your people "own" it and develop it.** Give employees the freedom to spend up to two to five days a year on the nonprofit of their choice. Being able to make their own decisions about where to invest their time makes it meaningful to them and they'll support it.
- **Use philanthropy to unite the company.** Consider doing team-building exercises around helping a favorite charity.

None of the practices above will end up costing that much, but you and your team will find that giving back to others is rewarding and well worth the effort.

Of course, if you want to dive in deeper, you can. I would wade in slowly here though, as people can feel so strongly about this that dialing anything back can lower morale. If you're ready to go all-in and create a comprehensive plan from the start, the Pledge 1% website will be a great resource.

I strongly believe that from the beginning of a company, it can have a soul. Caring about others less fortunate than us is soul food. I look forward to learning about how your company incorporates philanthropy into its DNA.

All the best,

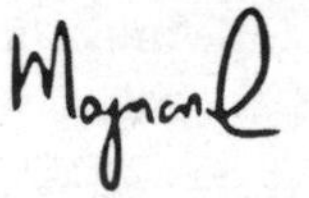

Maynard

PART II

GETTING TO RELEVANCE

3

Management Basics

WHEN YOU NEED TO DELEGATE

Dear Founder,

I am pleased to be discussing one of the most important ingredients for a leader's success: the art of delegation.

When you are very small and employ only two to three people, everyone has to pitch in, divide the tasks, and do the work. Even at that stage, it's likely that someone will take the lead on each initiative. For example, someone will take the lead on product, while someone else takes the lead on fundraising or sales. Delegation has naturally started to emerge.

When you start growing and are between ten and a hundred people, you will have to delegate more—and do it systematically and effectively. *Effectively* is the operative word here.

Too often, I've heard someone who has been given a task say, "I delegated that to X," and think that they're done. Not the case!

Years ago I had an amazing manager working for me who I could always count on to deliver what I wanted on time and on budget. Unfortunately, he was known as a micromanager, which made life difficult for the teams working for him. We therefore had to help him develop his "effective delegation" muscle, which we went to work on and we assumed things would improve.

Not long after, we had a "bet-the-company" project that we were running, and that manager (and his teams) played a major role. I stopped by to ask him how it was going, and he said very proudly, "I don't know, I've delegated it to the team—aren't you happy with me?" I wasn't.

Over years of managing teams, I have learned that *effective* delegation means that you know that the task/project will get done with the results that you expect. At the outset, this means that you have to:

- Assess the capability and willingness of the team to do the task. Often, people will volunteer for a cool assignment, but can/will they really do it?
- Communicate what success looks like to the people you are delegating to. What is the timeline, quality, etc.?
- Ensure they know that if they encounter problems, you are there to guide them. Overall, you are still accountable for the results. Delegation is not abdication.
- Establish checkpoints to monitor progress so you don't get any nasty surprises at the end.
- When the team delivers, celebrate their success.

The more confidence you have in a team or person, the less structure you need to make delegation work. However, if you haven't taught your team to fish, then it is often a recipe for disaster.

There is nothing more satisfying than seeing teams accomplish more than they (or you) thought possible, with minimum input or guidance from you. It frees up tremendous cycles for you to innovate or to lead in other areas. After all, effective delegation is a crucial building block for scale.

All the best,

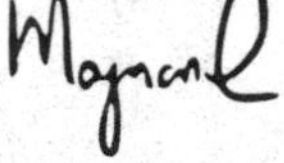

Maynard

WHEN YOU NEED TO KNOW WHO OWNS WHAT

Dear Founder,

We all have decisions to make every day. Successful decision-making isn't just about speed or outcome—it's really about empowering others to make the best decisions for the team.

To accomplish this, I use the RACI model. This system, which I learned when I was at Bay Networks, clearly articulates *who does what*. I have used this matrix for many years at big companies, where it helped clarify roles and responsibilities in cross-functional teams and projects. We use it today at WIN to determine everything from who owns the final decision on investments, to our PR strategy. It's become such a part of everything we do that it's now shorthand.

The first step in this model is to clarify what the decision is and when it has to be made. Write it down.

Then, you employ RACI, an acronym that delineates the necessary stakeholders in a decision. This outlines the person who is:

- **Responsible.** Who is the owner? Who sets the strategy? Who will decide? Ideally this should be one person, but it can be two. Remember, decision-making needs to be pushed down to the lowest competent level. If that's not done, it means you are not delegating enough. Worse, it means that you may be running a monarchy.
- **Approves.** Who will ratify or veto? This person is the one who delegates the work to the "R."
- **Consulted.** Who will be affected? These people do not have the right to make the decision, but you have the obligation to get their input before the decision is made, and you want to know what they have to say.

- **Informed.** Who has to be informed about the decision? Always err on the side of informing too many people rather than too few.

This model can help to make decisions faster and implement them more effectively because it helps to put aside internal bickering (which is often due to uncertainty about who owns what) and get on with the task of decision-making. This model helps provide role clarity, which can often be a source of tension. It will eradicate confusing debates, such as:

"This is my decision!"
"Not really."
"Oh, I am only a C or an I? I feel like an R."

RACI is an easy way to discuss and codify roles without having emotional battles.

The best decisions do not come from a majority vote or from a single authoritative voice. They are the result of something more balanced. The RACI model allows decisions to be made collaboratively, with the input of several voices and all the necessary data—but ultimately the answer is determined by a single decision maker who was tasked with this responsibility. This approach reduces unnecessary debate and enables timely decisions that are aligned with the company's priorities.

All the best,

Maynard

WHEN YOU'RE AFRAID YOU MIGHT BE A "TWEENER"

Dear Founder,

If you're reading this letter, you're probably struggling with your business strategy or execution.

At the risk of stating the obvious, here are two points to consider:

1. If things are really going well, and you're working on an investable business that's succeeding, it's very easy to decide to double down.
2. If your business is really doing poorly, and you don't see any signs of improvement you also have an easy decision: shut down, treat people well, and return as much cash as possible to shareholders.

Now for the nuance, and the more common situation I see: the tweener scenario. You're neither a breakout nor a complete failure. It's pretty easy to tell whether or not you're a breakout. It's not a matter of simply achieving any given metric, but rather that momentum is building and it's impossible to ignore. If you have a consumer-facing company, you can easily see if you've struck a nerve. If you have an enterprise company, people want to join your team, employees are thrilled, partners are talking about your technology, customers are huge fans, sales are outpacing the bandwidth of your team, investors are begging to give you money, infrastructure is melting. You know when you have it, and if you don't feel this (or feel it slightly), it means that you are not breaking out.

Okay . . . so what *is* happening? Your situation might be more that you have some customers, but the pipeline or the product is not robust enough to sustain rapid growth. You may be able to raise funds, but not be at preferable terms or with great investors.

Ask yourself the following questions:

- Do you get cold reach outs from the press, from investors, and from potential employees?
- Do your customers send notes about how much your product matters to them?
- Do people talk about you on social media?
- Are you honestly fulfilling a need better than anyone else?

If you say "NO" to the above, sadly you're in tweener territory. Now, what are your answers to the following questions?

- Do you still have to explain why your product matters?
- Do you find that huge success is always one release away?

If you answer "YES" to the above, you're in the danger zone.

In today's world, product-market fit happens faster than ever. When we invest, companies are often one to two years from actual product-market fit. And that's totally fine and normal. Yet if you are past that point, it might be worth asking your trusted investors if you look like a breakout. It could be an uncomfortable question, but they manage a portfolio of businesses, and they probably already have an opinion on the subject. And every quarter that passes where your business looks the same as it did three months before, is a quarter where breakout potential seems markedly lower.

Maybe you think being a tweener is okay. Maybe you think you can wait it out. You can't. The CEO of a tweener company needs to act with an incredible sense of urgency.

- You need to put strong plans in place to get back on track to become a breakout.
- You need to take a deep look at the current state of things and future projections with the board and management

team to assess how viable the strategy is and how bright the future looks. If some aspect of your business *is* working, consider betting the farm there. Often startups try to do too much and offer a "complete" solution, and that can slow their release schedule, make adopting their technology more onerous, and worst of all, dilute the quality of everything they offer.

- You may need to take significant actions (e.g., painful layoffs, redo of product, pivot, etc.) to ensure you have the cash needed to achieve the turnaround.

As an investor, I'm hopeful that all of my companies will be breakouts. But I know they won't all be. That's okay, because a couple breakouts make up for a lot of tweeners or failures. Yet as the CEO, you're spending all of your energy and time on this one idea. You need to ensure that it's going to return well for your employees, investors, and yourself.

If you are not convinced that you have a great chance of becoming a breakout, you should think seriously about M&A or returning cash to investors. I've watched companies burn through every penny without a plan or hope, and I've watched companies make a tough decision to return some money to shareholders and move on to something they more strongly believe in.

Expect this assessment to be one of the hardest you've ever faced. By now, you've invested years of human capital, money, and reputation into this business, and it can be a serious shot to the ego to admit it isn't working. Founders we back tend to be universally smart and driven, and many of them will never have faced something that feels so much like failure. But it isn't. Real failure is throwing even more time and capital at a business that isn't working, and ruining your chances to raise again down the line. Take the learnings, take the loss, take a vacation, and move on.

This is a long game. All of us want to be working on things that matter. I wish the same for you.

All the best,

Maynard

P.S. Please see the Appendix to this letter on the following page, which includes more clues as to whether you are in tweener-land.

APPENDIX

Still not sure whether or not you are a tweener? These are things we often hear in updates that set off the tweener radar:

- "We're working on our churn problem."
- "We're now working on [X new project]."
- "We published twenty thought pieces this quarter."
- "Our head of product/head of sales/head of marketing is leaving."
- "Our model [predicated on unfounded and aggressive assumptions] shows us earning 100x revenue in two years."
- "We weren't able to do [something we promised], because [competitor did something, team was slow, our big customer had a leadership change, and our sponsor left]."
- "We're working on technical debt."
- "We lost a big customer this month as their needs changed."
- "We grew 5% month-over-month."
- "Things are continuing with [three customers who are personal friends]."
- [No update]

WHEN YOU NEED TO SET GOALS

Dear Founder,

Goals are something that humans intrinsically need. From the very earliest days of starting your company, or launching any initiative, you set goals. Answers to basic questions like the ones below lead to clear and helpful goals for your business:

- How many people are we hiring?
- How much funding do we need?
- How long will our cash last?

Setting goals is natural and easy to do. Setting goals that are achievable, realistic, and inspirational is where the magic comes in.

I always start with this question: "What am I aiming for?" And, then I ask: "If we achieve it, will it matter?" Or, to paraphrase Steve Jobs, "Will it make a dent in the universe?"

Too often, I see goals that are achievable, but the bar is so low that the company doesn't achieve the *destiny* it's aiming for. (That scenario is definitely uninspiring for everyone involved.) Conversely, if the bar is too high and the team thinks the goals are unachievable, it won't really be committed to achieving the goals. (That scenario makes it impossible to get anything done.)

I am a perfectionist, so I want to achieve what I set out to do, but I also want to set goals that would be amazing—and challenging—to achieve. I've learned that it is better to aim very high and not quite achieve perfection than to nail every goal and deliver mediocrity.

This is the process that I use to help set and achieve goals:

Assess where the team is. Is it a high-performance team? How high performance? How does it operate?

Outline goals I'd be proud to achieve. What would I think is amazing?

Take a step back. Understand that very bold goals might intimidate the team. Teams that are not yet high performance will think they can't achieve aggressive goals. When goals are way out of range, you don't get the buy-in or commitment you need to make anything happen.

Reassess the goals. What would be acceptable to me and also make sense for the team? Look for the magic spot here—a goal that gives a little bit of angst (it's aggressive and inspiring), but is also realistic (it's achievable). Rather than set commits on next quarter, set them nine months out. People freak out in ninety days, but they are willing to set more aggressive goals for nine months out. With enough time, people think they can do anything.

Introduce these reassessed goals and a plan to the team. If you have done this right, the team will still find the goal aggressive, but also achievable. When I was at eBay around 2000–2001, we were at about half a billion in revenue, and Meg Whitman said she wanted us to reach $3 billion by 2005. It felt like when JFK said he'd put a man on the moon. Initially we didn't see a way to get there, but we figured out a plan and everyone came on board.

What's amazing is what happens after the team goes through some cycles where they successfully achieve these goals. Before long, the team starts learning to hit aggressive goals consistently. And then I've seen something even more incredible happen: They set and beat aggressive goals that exceed my expectations. I love nothing more than when I have to dial them back!

The sooner teams learn how to do things no one else imagined, the better everything works.

All the best,

Maynard

WHEN YOU NEED TO GIVE (AND GET) FEEDBACK

Dear Founder,

As a leader, it's your responsibility and obligation to help people improve and achieve their potential.

That means giving feedback is an important—and often difficult—part of your job. Thoughtful feedback may be a gift, but I find that people often don't see it that way. For this reason, leaders must deliver feedback in a way that the recipient will be open to receiving it. Some tips:

Praise in public; criticize in private. Always follow this rule. And remember, people are watching how you react. It's not just what you say, but how you say it and how you hold yourself.

Build trust. Do the necessary work in advance. People receive feedback better when they trust the person delivering it. Ideally, the recipient should understand that you're sharing thoughts in the interest of serving their needs. The more trust you can build, the easier it is to have more difficult discussions, because you come from a place of working together rather than a place of judgment. Additionally, if you know your employee's career aspirations, surfacing bad behavior can help them improve and achieve their own goals. The more trust you've built, the more candid you can be.

Give feedback constructively. When I started my career, I received feedback from *Mad Men*–style bosses who used feedback as a weapon to chastise. However, much like bullying, this approach has gone out of favor and is unlikely to yield great outcomes. Feedback should provide validation and inspiration. I've begun to see today's workplace is far more evolved than the one I grew up in—and that's a good thing.

Be thoughtful. Have everyone else's best interests at heart. Deliver feedback with love and good intentions. Don't hold these conversations when you're angry, because it's far more likely the recipient will feel hurt or judged—and thus defensive.

Understand where the person is. Feedback is best given when people are receptive. How do you know? Ask them. Say, "Do you have some time for a one-on-one? I had some suggestions I was hoping to share with you. If you are not prepared for that now, we can discuss when you are ready." Setting up the conversation in this manner is a way to clue them in to what is happening and to make them aware that you are here to help them. Recently, someone I work with wanted to vent, and I made it clear that I was not open to hearing it. Yet sometimes you have to let people get emotions out of the way and then get to a pragmatic discussion on what happened so you can help them gain perspective. You can do this with a simple, "This is what I am seeing. What do you see?"

Don't shy away from delivering feedback just because it's hard. We can't take the new nicer workplace to an extreme and let it remove our ability to offer constructive feedback. Tough love can go a long way on the path to improvement.

As a leader, you also have to understand the value of asking for and receiving feedback from the people with whom you work.

I've received lots of great feedback from Meg Whitman, and this input has changed how I worked with her and how I have approached leading others. One of her concerns was that sometimes she was just interested in brainstorming, but I would see the dialogue as an action item for myself. "I just want to have a discussion, that doesn't mean I want you to do it," she said. I had to learn how to slow down and collaborate rather than act like "Action Jackson."

Soliciting feedback is a great way for a top exec to learn and grow. Here are some tips on how to receive and ask for feedback:

Be a heat seeker for asking for feedback. Always ask, "Is this working? Is there anything else I should be doing?"

Be approachable and safe. It's hard for someone to tell you something critical, and it is important for you to be understanding that they may find it challenging. Try "baiting the hook"—you know some of your own weaknesses. Ask a colleague or direct report if they've noticed you do something you shouldn't, and if they have advice for you. Often, they will ask for advice in turn.

Start with an open mind. Try to understand where their advice is coming from. Even if you disagree, sharing feedback is hard and you should view their consideration as a gift.

Listen to what is being said. This doesn't mean you have to accept it, or do it, but you do need to listen.

You should not be afraid of truth. Commit to creating a learning environment and enlisting your team's support to help you grow—because every day you can be getting better. I promise that understanding that you're never done improving will help your career in spectacular ways.

All the best,

Maynard

WHEN YOU NEED TO HAVE AN OPEN DOOR

Dear Founder,

I am a huge fan of openness and transparency. I think founders and CEOs should be approachable. They should be open to engaging in dialogue, both inside and outside the company, and to soliciting feedback from employees, investors, and customers.

When you are starting out, I suggest that you give frequent updates to all employees. Such updates are ideally done in person, but can also be done in writing. The idea is to keep teams informed of your perspective and initiatives. This practice should also continue as you grow. Marissa Mayer gave weekly updates at Yahoo! called FYIs. At Salesforce, Marc Benioff hosts regular off-sites with his extended leadership team where he shares what's happening with the company and provides a forum to discuss and determine the direction.

You definitely want to be approachable and ensure that the culture doesn't "paper over" large issues. When you're small, you may not have an HR department to deal with tough issues, such as sexual harassment, discrimination, or bullying. This often means that these issues come to the CEO. Therefore, it's up to you that they get managed and handled correctly, either by you or by appropriate members of your staff.

You do not need to own and resolve each issue personally, but you do need to ensure that each issue gets resolved. Generally, it is best to have the person who has the issue work with their line management directly to resolve the problem (and not expect *you* to resolve the problem) and then report the resolution back to you.

Overall, you do want to have an open door. If you are not sure about what to do, always remember that your outside lawyers can be of service here. That's what they are there for and you must always make sure you are complying with all appropriate laws. (For example, the whistle-blower law, which requires you to not only investigate the situation but also protect the person raising the issue from retaliation.)

Of course, the more you have an appropriate tone at the top (see the letter "When you need to set the tone for appropriate behavior"), the easier and clearer all of this becomes. Most companies even install a "hotline" for issues that can be reported anonymously and without fear of reprisal.

All the best,

Maynard

Maynard

WHEN YOU NEED TO BE THERE FOR SOMEONE

Dear Founder,

There's a well-known saying that insists achieving success is mostly about showing up. Obviously, if you want to succeed you need to show up, but I've found that success really results from what you do once you're there. Showing you are committed, engaged, focused—and delivering great results—is what makes a difference.

The same goes for being there for someone. I've been involved with a lot of companies over a lot of years, and as a result, I've worked with a number of people and have seen a great deal of tragedies: deaths, divorces, addiction, suicides, and even murders. It's always painful to see someone go through something so difficult.

As an employer, you may be on the sidelines. Yet it's also your role, if possible, to get your people help. You may be a boss, but you are also human, and being there for someone is the most important thing you can do. I recently had someone close to me lose a loved one, and this experience got me thinking about the necessity of supporting an employee and a friend who is going through a challenging time, and about the best way to do this.

The first rule is to show up—even when it's difficult and you don't know what to say—and the next and more important step is to show that you really want to be there. That sounds obvious, but sadly it often doesn't happen. With everyone so busy, people frequently stay away in tough times. What people really need is for you to step up and lean in.

I have been the recipient of many people's invaluable support during the difficult times in my own life. I lost my father when I was just a kid, and I remember how people stepped up. My sports coaches, as well as other dads in the neighborhood, spent more time with me and offered me extra advice. They were sincere in showing that they cared and that really meant something to me. Later, when our daughter was hospitalized with a grave illness and had a grim prognosis, many of our coworkers jumped in and offered to help. They sent presents and cards, and several wished to visit (though they couldn't due to her being in the ICU). It was one of the most difficult times in my life, and the support of others around us sincerely helped my family through it.

When someone loses a loved one, or has a child who is very ill, it's important to demonstrate real care. Show compassion and relay your own experiences, because people can spot insincerity from a mile away.

Here's what you should be doing:

- First, ask if it is an okay time for the person to talk, in a quiet, nonstressed moment.
- Tell them you are sorry for their loss, or for what they are going through.
- Ask them if you can be of service or help in any way. When an event has been particularly devastating, I recommend just jumping in and helping. Volunteer to babysit their kids, ask if there's a foundation you can give to, offer to take work items off their plate.
- Just listen. In the cases of battling an illness or losing someone, learn more about this person who is so special to them.
- Help nourish them. Send food so they have less to think about and organize. Or send flowers to show you care.
- Ask them if you can check in again. Tell them that if they don't feel like talking, they don't need to answer the phone.
- Reassure them that you care and that everything at work is handled, and that there is nothing they should worry about. You should expect their productivity to fall, but I've found that tragic events can also bring out the best in fellow teammates.

Remember, as a manager, your behavior will also be what you hope your colleagues model. And in this case, the things that feel right to do for the person, are also the right things to do for your company.

Times of employee crisis.

It must be noted that there are times when you do not know what someone on your team is going through, but you know that something is wrong. That person also needs your help. There's a fine line between being helpful and supportive and overstepping.

- If you see that something isn't right, check in and ask. Do this early and often.
- You can't meddle, but you can show compassion and care. When you're worried about caring too much or stepping over a line, it's always better to be human and caring than to be perfectly correct.
- Try and get them the help they need, whether that means taking time off or helping them find and access the appropriate professional resources, which hopefully are covered in your company's benefit plan.
- Be aware that serious events can put a team through a collective depression. Determine what resources you can bring to bear to help the rest of the team.
- Be committed. Make people feel safe to share what they are going through and get professional advice along the way so you can be assured you are taking the right steps to help.

In order to be productive, your employees must be healthy and happy. If you see something is different with someone, check in and see how you can help. Yes, this may not be work-related, but it's life-related and it benefits everyone to try to help make everything work holistically.

It's always hard to see anyone go through tough times, but it's your responsibility to help see them through to the light. There's so much that's out of our control, but this one part is in our hands. What we do in these sensitive moments is important.

Remember, when a team member is going through catastrophic events it affects the whole team. You need to pay attention to them as well. Consider bringing in professional resources for the whole team to help guide them through.

All the best,

Maynard

Maynard

WHEN YOU NEED TO LEAD WITH INSPIRATION, NOT FEAR

Dear Founder,

Communication is so important. But it's not just what you say and how often you say it. It's also—perhaps even more so—about how you listen. Adhering to this practice is especially important when you're the CEO. It has massive implications for the culture you want for your company. Do you want to run your company based on fear and power, or based on inspiration? Stephen Covey famously advised, "Seek first to understand, then to be understood." A more folksy adage is that God gave us two ears and one mouth for a reason.

Listening is so important because not doing so comes off as defensive, and worse, it's a gating factor to success. I recently saw the danger of not following Covey's advice during a challenging communication with the CEO of one of our portfolio companies that's en route to being a breakout success. Although we've poured tons of energy and resources into the company's success, it has hit some self-inflicted turbulence. Though the turbulence isn't catastrophic, the company needs to course correct fast to live up to its full potential.

In a discussion with the CEO about the situation, it was my intent to gently make suggestions without telling him exactly what to do. I tried to articulate that I had spent time thinking about his problem, had seen a similar situation before, and wanted to help. Unfortunately, the CEO heard my counsel as criticism, which led to a debate with high emotions, rather than a collegial dialogue where everyone's views were heard.

Perhaps I was not overt enough, but I tried to be gentle in offering advice because I knew the CEO can sometimes get his hackles up when he perceives he is being challenged. This attitude is very out of character with how he usually shows up, in what I call good CEO behavior. This issue has unleashed a distressing problem for me: I've found myself not wanting to speak up or raise an issue because I feared it could lead to a debate or an argument. Having this concern has led me to hold back at times, especially with some smaller issues, but when I feel strongly about something I bring it up. As an investor, I have an obligation to call out any serious issue, and I need to do so in a way that is productive.

When a CEO frequently reacts to information or perspectives defensively, it sets off alarm bells for shareholders and board directors. If this is how the CEO reacts to people to whom they are accountable, how are they interacting with their employees? Do the employees feel safe in surfacing their concerns and ideas? By now, I've been through many battles, and I can handle a little turbulence. However, frankly, I find it to be tiring, no fun, and generally unnecessary. What concerns me WAY more than how a CEO hears my feedback, is whether they are actively listening to their own employees, customers, and shareholders.

I can't emphasize enough the power of active listening. Sometimes CEOs miss cues from advisers or employees because they're not listening carefully enough, they're not paying attention to nonverbal cues, or they're distracted by other things. That's not acceptable. Active listening is a skill all CEOs have to master in order to succeed with their board, their employees, their customers, and their community. A few ways to hone your listening skills:

- **Be open to others' thoughts.** Realize that everyone is entitled to their opinions and perceptions, even if you disagree with them.
- **Make sure you follow the Covey advice of seeking first to understand.** Keep asking questions until you have drained all the points the person hoped to make. If someone looks uncomfortable or attempts to change the subject, there is likely more on their mind. Make it safe for them to share their thoughts.

- **Ask clarifying questions.** Don't say judgmental things like, "You're wrong." Say, instead, "That's an interesting perspective, I need to think about it."
- **Don't act defensively or disregard what you've been told.** You can share your perspective, but at the end you should repeat what you've heard and have alignment around next steps to correct the situation.
- **Lead with inspiration, not fear.** If every discussion is a battle, people have to decide how much energy they want to expend and where, and you won't get engagement unless there's something really wrong. Replace a command-and-control culture with one that is inspiration based and gives everyone a chance to buy in and make meaningful contributions. The very best companies are led by inspiration—not by fear or power. Problems will happen at all companies, but people do their best work when their company's culture is based on getting the best from everyone, being open, celebrating problems and fixing them fast, and making everyone feel safe to help the company achieve its destiny.

Taking a step back, we all understand that as an entrepreneur you are a risk-taker who often has a contrarian point of view. As such, you are questioned constantly and need to have a chip on your shoulder in order to execute the vision. That's a strength. However, it becomes a weakness when you become so committed to your belief that you don't listen to what's not working and you aren't open to iterating and modifying your vision.

All the best,

Maynard

Maynard

WHEN YOU NEED TO BE OVERT

Dear Founder,

Are you surprised when your team sometimes does things or behaves in ways that are diametrically opposed to what you believe or hope that they will do? When you see such a situation occur, do you think that they should have known better since you've overtly communicated the expected behavior in such circumstances—maybe even several times?

At one point, I had a rock star executive who worked for me. She always got her deliverables done, but she left a lot of broken glass around her. She did things such as have 1:1s at midnight, which was insensitive to people's time and out of character for how we wanted to treat people. I addressed this time and time again with her. Since it never changed, I was worried that I wasn't being overt enough. Apparently, in this case, I was. She said, "I hear you, I just choose to do things differently." This eventually led to a parting of ways.

Yet other times, people aren't making their own choice; they simply aren't aware that their behavior isn't in step with your expectations. I was at an off-site for one of my boards recently, and there was discussion centered on how their manager scores had dropped from year to year on the "best places to work" score. In researching why, the company discovered that although everyone thought that managers were doing the basics such as having 1:1s, holding staff meetings, and giving feedback, many managers had actually not been doing them. The reason? *It had been assumed, but never overtly stated*. No one told the managers they had to engage in these practices and do them effectively. Managers weren't doing it simply because it hadn't been conveyed to them that it was important. Upon realizing this lack of communication, the company fixed it fast by stating the importance of these tools in everyone's plan and making sure every manager understood it was a priority.

I've been guilty of making the same "assumption" mistake. Not long ago I received a complaint at WIN that we didn't get back to a company with a response. I was surprised as not giving someone the dignity of a reply is totally out of phase with our values and how we want to treat people. After thinking that, I had to take a step back. I realized that I hadn't reiterated the importance of this behavior in a long time. I thought it was in muscle memory. I learned, though, I couldn't rely on that. This situation reminded me of the importance of constantly reiterating the message. The mistake provided a good chance to refresh the team on the importance of this behavior in an overt manner and I'm confident it won't happen again.

In a recent WIN dinner with Meg Whitman, she mentioned how she felt that when it came to values, if you think you're reciting them too much, it's still probably not enough. Information gets lost in complex organizations, and as the founder, one of your roles is to ensure the core messages of what you're doing, and what matters, are understood and echoed by everyone in your organization.

When behavior is at odds with expectations, do the following:

- **Decide whether the expectations of behavior have been communicated clearly and recently.** There is always a lot going on, and the most important things need periodic reinforcement.
- **If communication hasn't been done, now is a good time to start doing so.** Approach this calmly and professionally.
- **If communication has been done, figure out what's causing the split between your desires and the actual behavior.** Expectations may be unrealistic at times, but the behavior also may have deviated from expectations either because the expectation wasn't ingrained or because it was consciously disregarded.

When there's a disconnect—regardless of the root cause—it's up to you to correct it. Own your part to ensure that communication will be done effectively and repeatedly. Take steps to make the expectations overt and hold people accountable.

Also, be realistic. Understand that you can't make EVERYTHING matter. If you try to be overt on everything, you'll pummel the team to death. Instead, decide what trumps what. Let everything else go, and be overt about what matters most.

All the best,

Maynard

WHEN YOU NEED TO FIND SYNCHRONICITY

Dear Founder,

Recently I was having a really bad day. A new employee quit unexpectedly and all of a sudden I had a huge problem on my hands. I went to a meeting with one of our CEOs and at the end of the meeting we spent a few minutes talking more about business and life. I shared my current crisis with him—I was looking for a new executive assistant again—and he responded that his wife used to work with a recruiter for EAs and they'd be on the lookout for potential candidates for me. He then told me that his wife was struggling to fill a head of compensation position and asked if I knew anyone. As luck would have it, I knew the CEOs of two compensation consultant firms that work with many compensation executives and I said I would be happy to put them in touch.

I left the meeting in awe of the synchronicity that just happened. He had insightful solves to a problem he didn't know I had and I had helpful answers to his wife's problem. None of these would have surfaced if we had not gone beyond what we were expected to discuss and asked other questions.

Synchronicity is about seeing around corners—and it's necessary when doing something as tricky as building a business. Too often we expect to find the answers we need from sources we know, but there are answers to questions everywhere. It's necessary to have a learner's mind and to be open to input and insight from everywhere. A few ways to see around corners:

- Identify what's troubling you. You must be super-aware of the problem you are trying to solve.
- Be open to gaining insight from everywhere.
- Sometimes this means doing something uncomfortable. Be willing to walk out of your comfort zone.

- Ask probing questions to those around you.
- Delve into how you can solve someone else's issues.
- When synchronicity happens, seize it.

Synchronicity may sound like a simple thing, but I promise you it can unleash something incredible and answer your most complex problems. I know this firsthand. When I was named the COO of eBay I was tasked with defining "culture" at the company. After an exhaustive effort, the entire program went off the rails. I was distraught over the situation and knew that I had to do something exceptional to get things back on track.

At that moment a book called *Radical Change, Radical Results* arrived. As it happened, my wife and the kids were out of town so I spent the weekend reading it. It was as though the authors Kate Ludeman and Eddie Erlandson had been observing some of our cultural issues at eBay. In the pages they wrote, I found solutions to my conundrum. I was amazed. I reached out to thank them, but something else happened. Meg Whitman (mostly to humor me) agreed to have Kate and Eddie do 360s for the two of us. Though she was initially ready to kill me for talking her into this, she loved it. I also learned a tremendous amount and it led to a much bigger and better cultural exercise at eBay and ignited a whole new set of values and ultimately a rebirth of the culture at the company. That initial work led to a long-term relationship with these coaches, which strongly influenced the course of my life. Kate showed me that my underdog persona was not very helpful anymore. With her prodding, I started doing fireside chats, which eventually led me to writing my own book, and to co-founding Everwise.

I love hearing other people's stories of synchronicity. Consider Marc Benioff's. When he started Salesforce, he didn't initially share his idea with a lot of people, but over lunch, his friend Bobby Yazdani, the founder of Saba Software, encouraged him to, saying that the number one mistake entrepreneurs make is holding their ideas too closely to the chest. Marc considered that and shared with Bobby what he wanted to do. "It's very good you told me," Bobby said, and then introduced him to three contractors he had working for him who soon became Marc's co-founders and helped him build an incredible service and company. In fact, Marc has described meeting Parker Harris, one of those developers, as "the luckiest thing in my life." That's synchronicity and it happened because Marc articulated his vision and shared it with someone who had experience, understanding, and a desire to help.

Synchronicity happens more often than we know. Look for it everywhere and you will see what it can do.

All the best,

Maynard

WHEN YOU WONDER IF NETWORKING OR MARKETING EVENTS ARE WORTH YOUR TIME

Dear Founder,

As a founder, there are great demands for you to be with your team running your company, but sometimes getting out is exactly what your company (and you) may need.

If you're extroverted, the thought of attending an event may energize you. If you're introverted, as I am, the thought may stress you out and cause you to want to avoid it. I am a believer in the power of the right events to accelerate your business and give you some fresh perspective. When approached correctly, events can allow me to do three weeks' work in just a few hours. They also provide a great opportunity for synchronicity.

That said, my general aversion for events has gotten me into trouble in the past. For years at WIN, I felt strongly that we shouldn't host a conference of our own. Eventually, my team convinced me otherwise, and we hosted a day-and-a-half-long summit for all of our founders and affiliates, and I left a convert. The energy was incredible. We enabled dozens of new connections, created sessions so founders and affiliates could directly open up about their learnings, and everyone left with a better idea of what makes our firm special. Achieving the same ends through one-off meetings would have taken a year.

IF YOU ARE ATTENDING AN EVENT

Don't do it all. There is only so much time we all have. Decide which events make sense, and guard your time religiously. Similarly, do not go to every session at each event. At Dreamforce, Salesforce's annual user conference, I always go to the keynotes and leave the rest of my schedule open for serendipity.

Plan some meetings in advance. People have busy schedules, especially with the compressed time of an event. Get an attendee list and put meetings on the calendar before you go so you won't miss the opportunity to see each other.

Have fun, but measure results. Events are not just about partying, though that does seem to define some of them. Make sure you keep what matters at the top of your mind: new insights and new connections. I make sure that attending an event will enable me to make at least twice the impact I would have had in the office, and I define what that looks like so I know how to focus my time at the event. Define what a successful event looks like for you in advance, and then chase your goals while there. Also remember to leave some time that isn't scheduled (see the "When you need to find synchronicity" letter). Frequently, I've come up with some new insights or ideas while listening quietly to someone else speak.

Be measured. In the tech industry in particular, there can be a temptation to go down the path of becoming a "celebrity founder," where every week you might be talking at a different event. It can be very easy to justify this time allocation as each conference will bring new business cards that look like progress, but I often find these to be unsustainable methods. New sales leads should mostly come from a healthy sales org, not the CEO attending dozens of events. Further, always being on the road can be toxic for the company at home. You can miss major problems and if your company hits a hiccup or setback, the backlash can be catastrophic. If many events are important to attend, consider elevating some of your team members in your stead; it's amazing experience for them, and it will let you cover a lot more ground.

IF YOU ARE HOSTING AN EVENT

Think carefully about who attends. You need to make sure you have the right mix of people. Don't make the invite list too big—it should not be a cast of thousands, but an intimate event of the right caliber of people. Marc Benioff masterfully creates the right mix of attendees, which includes customers, prospects, team members, board members, journalists, philanthropists, and a few other interesting people. Sometimes this includes a musician or magician. It keeps things interesting!

Build in informal time for interaction. Leave room for surprises. Events that are hosted somewhere other than the office or conference center are a great way to get people more invested and present. The most meaningful encounters happen when people are at an event for a dedicated period of time, not just popping in for one topic that interests them. That's because relationships are not built during formal programming, but rather when people have an opportunity to create the conversation in a comfortable atmosphere. (At the Upfront Summit, a big technology event in Los Angeles, most of my best "meetings" took place around the food trucks that served lunch.) Make sure there are spots for mingling so attendees are not all running back to their hotel room to hide (or do email).

Make sure people want to come back. That means ensuring that every attendee leaves with more than they expected. Build a roster of impactful content and give them opportunities to have fun (I find contests help with this) to help make them feel like the event was worth their time—including the cost of travel and time away from the family.

So, introverted or extroverted, attending conferences should make it to your priority list. Like everything else, though, you need to manage them wisely and ensure you get the return expected for the time spent. And, by the way, have some fun along the way and bring the learnings back home to the team!

All the best,

Maynard

Maynard

WHEN YOU NEED TO BUILD YOUR ALUMNI NETWORK

Dear Founder,

When you lose a talented individual, it hurts. I remember that in the early days of eBay (and several other companies), when someone left, we often reacted with a cold shoulder—as it felt like we had been rejected.

That was wrong. This attitude is wrongheaded. I have to thank John Donahoe for helping us change this attitude. John was the former CEO of Bain who later became the CEO of eBay and is now the CEO of ServiceNow. Bain had an amazing alumni network that they nurtured. It was so effective that we've since tried to implement it elsewhere.

The fact is, we don't own our people; they choose to work for us and we choose to hire them. It is our obligation to do everything we can to make them better while they are with us. It is the employee's obligation to do everything they can to make the company successful.

When someone decides to leave—whether the employer decides the employee no longer is needed or the employee decides they no longer want to work there—we should be thankful and appreciative on both sides. We should agree to stay in touch.

In many ways, I created the Webb Investment Network in order to stay in touch with colleagues as I transitioned out of my operational role and into my role as an investor. It is a source of constant energy and joy to see the network grow, have fun, and contribute resources and guidance to our portfolio companies.

There is even one affiliate in our network who claims I fired him (I didn't; I think he left on his own accord), but we stayed on good terms. I invested in his new company, which he eventually sold to

Yahoo! He has been an amazing addition to the network, which is something I did not imagine when we parted ways in 2008.

Here are some steps you can take to stay in touch with alumni and build your network:

- Send every team member off well. Thank them for their service and solicit their willingness to stay in touch.
- Create an alumni page on Facebook or LinkedIn. Keep an in-house contact list.
- Periodically create content to update alumni on the latest goings-on at the company. Include things they may be able to help you with, such as suggesting candidates for a job opening.
- Be willing to show up at alumni events. You might want to even consider hosting them.
- Make everyone feel that they are still in the family even though they've left the house!

An alumni network can be an amazing source of referrals for candidates and new business. Even more importantly, though, it's a source of validation for the people who have been a part of your company's journey.

All the best,

Maynard

WHEN YOU NEED TO BUILD A GREAT BOARD

Dear Founder,

Congratulations! You are officially a real company. Well, you've been a real company, but now you've raised outside money—and you'll likely have to put together a formal board.

Caution!

If at all possible, stay informal—do not have a formal board for as long as possible. One of our biggest breakout companies has a "board of one," and the founder jokes about holding an annual board meeting in the Caymans, where he talks to himself. At WIN, I made the decision to self-fund for exactly this reason—I am accountable to myself and not to anyone else (except my wife).

However, let's look at this realistically: Unfortunately, most founders don't have the immediate success or funds to enable them to forgo outside money. If you've raised outside money, is it possible to get your first round without having to formally establish a board? If so, I strongly recommend going this route. I suggest having periodic meetings with key investors and running those meetings as though they were board meetings, but with none of the other members having voting authority and control. (See the letter "When you've just raised your first round of funding.") Adopting such a strategy keeps you in charge, and it also serves as a good litmus test; it gives you a chance to see how much someone is contributing and how well they interact with you.

Most likely, if you build a successful business, you won't be able to get away without building a formal board for long. And when it comes time to creating a board, you will find that it is one of the most pivotal decisions you will make in your entire career.

Why? Ask most board members what their number one job is, and they will most likely say it's hiring or firing the CEO. Board members will cover all kinds of other things—providing strategic insight, opening doors, advice and counsel, and all of the regulatory obligations that come with being a public company—but they will always say their number one job is to ensure they have a great CEO in place.

So, for a founding CEO (or any CEO), building a great board is essential to your company's success (not to mention your own personal success). While selecting an investor based on terms alone is understandable, in the long term it's more important to prioritize the person (and firm) and the impact they can have instead of the price offered.

When I was being recruited as the CEO of LiveOps, I was very clear that I would want to build a different board, and I negotiated the ability to do that as part of my transition. We selected an offer for a Series C from a very trusted person and source—even though it wasn't the best financial offer. Chemistry is crucial and selecting the right board for the new direction of the company made all the difference in achieving what we set out to do.

Some things to keep in mind when building and working with a board:

Choose small boards over big boards, especially in the early days of your startup.

Less is more! Keep your board as small as possible. Build hands-on boards with members who are willing to help and provide advice, rather than board members who are trying to play "smartest person in the room." It's important to ensure that the board is engaged and treated with appropriate dignity and respect.

Just as you are always assessing the talent that is on your team, you should be assessing the talent that is on your board.

What help do you need now, and what will you need when you are much bigger? There are some seats (like investor seats) that are guaranteed, but most times board seats can be swapped, and changes should be made so that the best person possible is in every seat.

Select board members who fill your gaps.

I always selected members based on some of my weak areas. I didn't have extensive sales and marketing experience, so I added someone who had been a CMO of a big public software company and a sales exec at Hewlett-Packard. Some seats are directly attached to functional expertise, such as the head of the audit committee. I always tried to select someone who could excel at that role, but who was also interested in helping more strategically. If possible, put someone in an "adviser" role first so you can see how you interact.

Understand why someone wants to be on your board.

What are the motives for joining the board? Sometimes the best way to become CEO is through a board seat. Sometimes board members still want to run companies. Others want some ego gratification. None of these are good reasons. Most people who are eligible for boards are very accomplished, but you need to know whether they want to provide advice and counsel—or whether they want to do operations. Are they willing to be one voice of five? Or would they rather have everyone do what they say? Board members wield a lot of power and it's very difficult to get someone off. Choose the right individuals who want to be of *service.*

Pursue people who don't want to be on a board.

This suggestion sounds strange, but it is perhaps my best tip. Busy people with big jobs are great selections because they won't spend all their time obsessing over your company (but make sure they will be willing to be available when you need them). Someone with a lot of free time might want to spend it with you—you don't want that. I've found that often the people who talk the most and demand the most are of the least value.

Instead of dreading board meetings and seeing the members as "overhead," put these great resources to work for you.

The importance of having a close collaboration with the board is one of the most valuable things I learned as a CEO. I always took my biggest issues to the Board, sought their input, and then made my decision. Make meetings a source of affirmation and insight. Put the board to work on lead generation, problem-solving, and pattern recognition. Advice from seasoned veterans can also help you grow and operate as a manager and leader.

Make allies, not enemies.

Appreciate the board in the best of times, so they are there for you in the worst of times. Board meetings and board assignments can either be very tedious and boring (when things are really going well), or very intense and crazy (when things are stalling or in flux). When everything is going well and the CEO and company meet or exceed goals, it is often easy to be a little arrogant with your board and see them as overhead. Don't do that. Having great chemistry and trust is very important, because when the tide changes (success is not usually linear), you want the board to feel informed and eager to help you.

It is my fervent hope that you end up building a great board, one that helps make your company and you stronger and one with which you enjoy spending time. As with everything, it's all in your control!

All the best,

Maynard

4

Management Challenges

WHEN YOUR FIRST KEY HIRE LEAVES

Dear Founder,

I'm sure you're somewhere between being pissed off that you are being deserted, and worried about what you're going to do to make up for this person's contributions. Maybe you're even more concerned that this will be the start of an avalanche: *How many more people are thinking about leaving?*

TAKE A DEEP BREATH. If you become as successful as I hope you will, this departure will be the first of many people who will leave over time. It always hurts when a key contributor leaves.

Before I give you my recommendations, let me start with a fun and true story.

Two co-founders of one of our successful breakout companies asked to meet me to discuss a serious HR problem. They said that one of their early stars had now turned into a big performance problem. They wished they could fire him, but there was an issue: His dog was universally loved by everyone. The founders thought people would really be bummed to see the dog go. My advice: Fire the employee and keep the dog! I was just kidding, but I was serious that they needed to address the problem. (They did; the dog left, too, but someone brought a new dog in, and many years and hundreds of employees later we still laugh about the story.)

My advice for when you are about to lose someone who means a lot to the organization:

- **Find out why they are leaving.** Are they running away from something or running toward something? Do they have their heads on straight regarding the situation?
- **Are they salvageable?** If there is something wrong, can you fix it?

- I always use additional compensation as a last resort, as it's usually not compensation that makes someone want to leave.
- If you can fix it, is the person mature enough to recommit and be wholly engaged?

- **If you think they are salvageable, still do a gut check and make sure you're not getting gamed.** Sometimes people use the threat of leaving as a way to angle for more money. Unfortunately, people sometimes do disingenuous things. I have experienced situations where people have lied about the size of a job offer. You want to give people the benefit of the doubt, but you do have to be careful as you do not want to build an entitlement culture where people think that if they threaten to quit, they become eligible for a promotion. This will make costs go crazy and will render you powerless. Reserve the times you are willing to go through heroics for 1% of the employee population—the true talent—not 30–50% of the people who are trying to get a better offer. Everyone knows what's happening and you have to be mindful about how they view your response. If you are not careful, soon everyone will be at your door with a counteroffer and a request for a raise and promotion. How can you tell what's what? Probe where they are going. Then tell them that it sounds like a great opportunity, and that if it doesn't work out, they are welcome to come back.
- **If they definitely will be leaving, can you negotiate a transition plan that's beneficial for both of you?** Can you get their agreement to help out in a pinch even if they are in a new job?
- **Treat them with respect and dignity on the way out.** Celebrate their contributions and let them know they are welcome back if things don't work out where they are going.

- **But remember, you need to celebrate the people who stay and do good work as much as—or more than—the folks that leave.** I've heard people say they only got recognized when they left (the squeaky wheel gets all the grease syndrome), which leads to very bad cultural dynamics.
    - Make sure the team knows that the departing person will be missed, but talk about the actions you can take and they can take to ensure the company will still achieve its dreams.
    - Recognize that this is a great opportunity for someone else to step up and get a promotion.

- **Finally, look back and assess whether losing this person was a surprise.** Did you see it coming? Make it a point to proactively know where all your key talent stands—and work hard to keep them motivated and in the game.

I know it's a big loss and a big hassle to have to deal with a key hire departing. However, it's totally normal and manageable. Get through the pain quickly and elegantly, and get yourself back to terra firma as fast as possible.

All the best,

Maynard

WHEN YOU HAVE TO FIRE AN EMPLOYEE FOR THE FIRST TIME

Dear Founder,

I am very sad that you find yourself in this situation. Most people truly do not like to inflict pain and discomfort on someone else, which is what happens when you take someone's job away from them.

I was interviewed for my first management job at IBM when I was in my late twenties. My boss's boss asked me if I could fire someone and I replied, "Yes, but I will never have to." He laughed in my face and asked me why. I explained that I felt that most people wanted to do a good job, and that with the right coaching and the right manager they would blossom. (Somehow, I still got the job.)

Well, a few decades later, I've personally had to fire a fair share of people—thousands if you count organizations that I managed. It's never fun, but it's almost always necessary.

Organizations, even small startups, have great performers as well as people who aren't so great. Big companies are notorious for having mediocre people. Startups can't afford this. As a founder, you have to view each employee as someone you are giving something very precious to—like a ticket to the Super Bowl on the fifty-yard line. You're hopefully going to change the trajectory of this person's life, and in doing so, you need to hold them accountable to achieving the company's potential.

Too often, we accept mediocrity. I routinely ask leaders to look at their teams and decide how many of their people they would hire again if they had an open position. Sadly, the number is rarely above 80%. Remember, performance is not a static thing. Someone may be a great performer early and then check out later. Or their role or priorities may shift over time. The best cultures require outperformance at all times, and if something starts to go south, take steps to correct it quickly.

The fact is, most people wait too long to fire someone. That's a problem because most great performers become very frustrated having to deal with the results of working with second-rate performers. They expect that good managers and leaders will not allow for this situation to continue, and they will applaud it being resolved as long as it is done humanely.

How do you know when it's time to let someone go? By the time you start worrying about it, it's probably too late. I estimate that in 80% of the instances where someone starts wondering if an employee will measure up, they never will and they will not stay for long at the organization. Of course this also means that sometimes it might work out. Therefore, be very crisp on what has led you to question their chance of success in the role. Determine the driving issue of your concern: Are they not making the commitment? Are they not working hard enough?

Once you have that clarity, you have to assess:

- **If they are recoverable.** Go all-in and try to help. Expect them to make it, but simultaneously work on your recovery plans in case it will not work. (If you've read the letter "When you need to recruit," you already know the value of looking before there's an opening.)
- **If it's not fixable.** Go into "dead man walking" mode. Treat everyone nicely, continue to ask them to deliver and put more checkpoints in place, but don't invest in preserving them in this role any longer. It is only a matter of time before they will be leaving the organization. Act in a way that will minimize damage.

Here are my recommendations:

- **Do not put this off.** The situation has to be addressed immediately.

- **Project how it will be on the other side of this difficult process.** I've always found that thinking about firing someone was far worse than the actual act of doing so.
- **Look back. Have you done your job to set the person up for success?** If so, keep moving. If not, do you think that you can effectively set them up for success? And are you and the team willing to try? If so, put the person on an improvement plan with clear expectations and checkpoints. If not, again, keep moving, but next time do a better job of setting your people up for success.
- **Treat the person well on the way out.** Be firm on why they are being let go, but explain what you are doing to help them. Let them resign if they desire, and still give them whatever severance you were prepared to give them after firing them. Let them propose (subject to your review and approval) the messaging around their departure. Some people may prefer it to look like they voluntarily resigned. Let them opt out.
- **Understand that how you treat employees who are being fired or placed under performance review is important, and will be remembered by all members of the company.** Not only are your employees aware of what's happening, they are all projecting themselves in a similar situation. A long time ago, I had a boss who was fast and furious when it came to firing people. One time, he fired one of my employees so quickly—and without telling me—that the guy ran out, leaving his boots behind in his desk drawer. Don't go into "smoking boots" mode. It creates lots of drama, leaves a big gap you have to fill, and introduces a lot of fear. Remember, how you fire people carries repercussions for everyone else. Use the Golden Rule and treat everyone the way you'd like to be treated—even, and especially, on the way out.

- **Think about what you will say as a reference—and talk about it.** Having this kind of dialogue is a good way to ensure a smooth transition.
- **After it's done, be open with your team.** Be willing to answer questions without disparaging the individual.
- **Find someone great to fill the role being vacated.** As difficult as it is to let someone go, understand that this is a great opportunity for someone else. Give one of your stars a chance to take it on. Throughout my career, I've been more pleasantly surprised with "battlefield promotions" than by hiring rock stars from outside. I've always had more success by promoting from within rather than hiring from the outside. Give someone on the team the chance to step up and to learn and grow.
- **Commit to doing even better on the next hire.** If the person didn't work out, it's not just their fault. It's your fault, too. You hired someone who wasn't right. What are the signals and learnings for you to make sure you're hiring right the next time?

Let me end where I started: I'm sad that you have to go through the difficult process of having to fire someone. However, I'm also glad that you're stepping up to it—it's one of the most important pieces of your job, and one that too often is not done very well.

All the best,

Maynard

WHEN YOU NEED TO GAIN CREDIBILITY

Dear Founder,

You already know a great deal about credibility. You've already developed enough credibility with investors to get funded and with your employees to develop a staff.

But that's just the start. You are either gaining or losing credibility—and building or eroding trust—every day.

Take, for example, this recent scenario. One of our portfolio companies just missed its quarter badly. Their head of sales was trying to convince the board to lower quota from what was agreed in the plan, and I noticed that the employees in the building all seemed quite content. No one thought missing the quarter was a big issue. I was concerned about the laissez-faire attitude and I mentioned it to the CEO and the head of sales, who escalated it to a fire drill. The next thing I knew, everyone quickly became busy, but no one was accomplishing what mattered.

With this experience, I learned—yet again—to not speak casually and offhand. My comments had been heard, but I had not been specific enough about what to do. If you are in this situation, you have to ask what you can do to fix the situation and reestablish trust:

1. What are the concrete actions you can take to lead the company to a better place?
2. What do you need to help achieve them?
3. When will these actions be done?

A few things to consider:

- **Determine if your strategy and plan inspires confidence or fear.** Does it tell a breakout story and show you are being as proactive as possible, or does it tell a defensive story (e.g., huddle down, preserve cash, and hope for product/market fit)? If you don't inspire confidence, don't expect trust to build.

- **Do you deliver on promises made (what I call "do what you say and say what you do")?** Staying true to your word is essential. If you are not carrying through on your commitments, do you know why, and are you taking the appropriate steps to course correct?
- **Is your response effective?** I have often seen people taking the wrong actions and doing things with a "false urgency." (See, for example, what happened in the scenario with the head of sales above.) In his book *A Sense of Urgency,* John Kotter postulates that most individuals and companies live in a "complacency zone." However, when they are faced with challenges, Kotter writes that they often create "hair on fire" task forces, which exhibit false urgency rather than true urgency—the kind that inspires people and really moves the needle. Leaders must only work on what makes a real impact.
- **Don't confuse action for traction.** Realize that just because you're busy, it doesn't mean you're making forward progress. You have to focus on the right things. It's necessary to organize and prioritize in order to achieve the right outcomes. How do you do that?

    - Iterate and test your way into knowing what success really looks like.
    - Once that is clear, double down, move fast, and execute.

For entrepreneurs, there's no shortage of working hard, but you need to assess your efforts to examine whether or not you are working on what matters, what inspires everyone around you, and what builds their trust in you.

All the best,

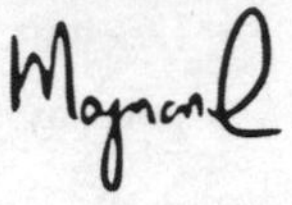

Maynard

WHEN YOU NEED TO UNDERSTAND THE IMPACT YOUR JUDGMENT IS HAVING ON YOUR DECISIONS

Dear Founder,

As a CEO, you have to make judgments all day long. I would argue that the same is true in our personal lives. We also are constantly making snap judgments: that person is a bad driver, a lousy planner, a crummy cook. (There's plenty of interesting material on this topic—check out *Blink* by Malcolm Gladwell.)

While making fast judgments can be detrimental in your personal life, they are especially consequential in your job, where you can dramatically impact someone's career and livelihood. Think about it: You make a hiring decision based on judgment, and you use the same judgment to decide on a career promotion or a raise. It comes into play with everything: which strategy should we chase, which product should we build, which person do we promote?

Understanding the role that our judgment plays is a really complicated issue. Sometimes we think we are making decisions with the appropriate facts, but we all have powerful, always-running unconscious cognitive biases that affect our decisions. And our brains can behave completely differently in different contexts. Our biases may lead us to hire someone that acts like us or seems familiar and they may cause us to stay away from something we don't know or don't understand.

None of this means that we should shy away from making decisions. We simply must understand that our judgments will always be fast and imperfect and therefore we must do everything in our power to build some process and transparency for our decision-making. Here's what to keep in mind so you can keep a clear and fair mind before you make a decision:

- Don't ever fret about whether you have to make decisions. Fret about whether you are doing them without quick judgments and with an open mind—that will dictate the best thing to do.
- Conduct decisions with an air of wonder. Ask yourself: *Do I have all the facts I'd like to have? Am I missing anything?* (You always are.) *Are there subconscious biases creeping in?* Ask: *Have I thought of everything else?* and go back and reconsider.
- Ask others for their opinions on what they would do if they were you. Make sure you are not insular on who to ask—don't gloss over people you are pretty sure will disagree with you. Think about how anyone else in your circumstances would respond and what they would decide. Don't be afraid of asking for help if you don't know the answer. Go to your board, employees, or peers. Gathering input from others is often helpful and doesn't mean you will not ultimately make the decision. And the real mastery comes when everyone else thinks they made the decision, but in reality you did.
- Determine if this decision is one that you have to make. If someone else can do it, that's good; it's an opportunity for them to hone their judgment. You should always be working to empower your people to make crucial decisions. (See the letter "When you need to know who owns what.")
- Decide. Understand the time constraints of the decision and proactively decide whether to make a decision or not. Does the situation require an answer now? If so, make it. Too many people delay making decisions. That is, in essence, making a decision.
- Hone your judgment so that you keep getting better. If you make a decision that isn't right, learn from it. Be willing to admit when you've made a mistake. Acknowledge your error and fix it fast. Consider adding a postmortem process

> for key decisions: Were they good or bad? What information should you have gotten? Judgment tends to gets easier with experience and practice, though keeping an open, inquisitive mind often becomes harder.

We all must realize that we are all applying judgment, every day. Do your best to have pure and transparent motives, which will help you make fair and better judgments and clear and sound decisions.

All the best,

Maynard

WHEN NO ONE IS EXCITED TO BE HERE

Dear Founder,

You can feel energy in rooms. It's palpable. It radiates. When teams are energized, everything seems way more possible to achieve.

On your best days, your people feel how the Philadelphia Eagles felt after the Super Bowl or how the Warriors felt after winning the NBA championship. On a scale of 1 to 10, they feel like a 10. On the other hand, reducing the workforce by half or cutting everyone's pay makes them feel pretty different. That's a 1.

If you're reading this letter, you may be having a lot more "1" days than "10" days. I'm sorry that the spirit seems to be gone from your team. There's nothing worse than feeling an energy gap among your people.

Here's the truth: It's up to you as the leader to set the tone for what energy is expected. *You* have to set that example and exude that kind of energy.

A few tips to get your team more energized and enjoy better days ahead:

- **First calibrate where you are.** What's the highest energy level your team has ever had? Have you had a "10" day? What's an average day like? What's today?
- **Celebrate the wins that exist.** Do fun things with your team. Take a break to treat your team to a movie, or do some charity work together. It can be simple: At LiveOps we had random Nerf arrow attacks and paper airplane contests; at AdMob and Everwise, the sales team rang a gong when a big deal was done. It's especially important to do this when times are hard. When I first joined eBay, nothing was working. Nine days after I started we did a free listing day, where normal fees were lifted for twenty-four hours. The commu-

nity loved it—they stayed up all night posting listings and this promo sparked such an increase in volume in one day that it put us a year ahead on volume projections. While the free listing event was a great marketing ploy for the company, it was a nightmare for the people running the system. We worked tirelessly, made it through the capacity problems, and then shared a collective sigh of relief. We had a parade throughout the building to thank everyone, and this activity turned the relief into positive energy.

- **Honor special occasions.** Welcome everyone and celebrate every new hire. Acknowledge special occasions such as anniversary dates. IBM used to give a gold watch to celebrate twenty-five years with the company, but most people don't stay so long with the same company anymore. You don't have to wait twenty-five years! You can celebrate every year, and other milestone anniversaries, in small ways by recognizing people's achievements in all-hands meetings or by writing them thank-you notes.
- **Treat setbacks as learning experiences.** If there are problems, address them candidly and openly. Let people ask questions and then enlist their support to fix things.
- **Personally model the enthusiasm—even when it's hard.** At eBay, some days were hard and even without saying a word, people could tell that I was troubled by something. They got worried and asked what was wrong. I would say, "Wow, just because I wasn't smiling you think I'm angry, or someone is in trouble." However, I had to accept that my actions were leading them to worry. I had to maintain more of a sense of calm, even in an urgent situation. I learned that from Meg Whitman's leadership. She made me laugh every day, and these interactions helped me get through the clutter. As a leader, you need to model courage, candor, and resolve.

- **Spend time engaging with people.** Say hello to them in the morning and good-bye at night. Be approachable. Ask about their families and show them you care about things other than getting their work done. When they miss work because their baby is sick, ask about how the child is doing when they come back. Also, enable your teams to enjoy and get to know each other. One great and very simple way to do this is through team lunches and dinners.
- **Extend inclusion beyond your employees.** It's important to include the families. People work hard and their families miss them when they're away—you need to enlist loved one's support, as well. Include them in special events. At eBay, Meg took every vice president and above away for a weekend with their families. Being able to share an experience together resonated greatly with employees and their families.

I'm sorry your team isn't that energized. When things are tough, it's time for leadership to be more present and demonstrate how to get through this bump to better days ahead. Step up into this role and don't let the team bring you down—you need to lead them to greatness!

All the best,

Maynard

WHEN YOU NEED TO DEAL WITH POOR PERFORMERS

Dear Founder,

It happens all the time: someone looks great on paper, stands out in an interview, and then joins the company—and then things don't go according to plan. Their skills aren't really a match, their experience isn't translating, and they are not achieving what they were tasked to do. These are issues that every entrepreneur battles. In fact, some studies show that hires don't work out 50% of the time. A few things to consider when faced with an employee's poor performance:

Investigate always. As a leader, it is your responsibility to do everything you can to understand the reason behind poor performance. Determine why the employee is struggling. Are they not able to give their full attention? Do they no longer like their job? Have a conversation with the person and get input from the executive team and the board to determine the appropriate next steps.

Set expectations of excellence and make sure there is clarity on all sides. Expectations must be set high, and must be both aggressive and achievable. With aggressive goals, hitting 80% of them is amazing, but hitting 100% of goals means you likely didn't set the bar high enough.

Communication is key. Be crisp and clear with the individual on what they must do to get better.

Establish a culture that allows people to ask for help early and often. Problems are good. If made aware of them early, you can solve them.

Fix it fast. If problems do not get better, sometimes other actions are necessary. Remember, by the time you are aware of poor performance, your superstars are already aware of someone not pulling their weight. They are counting on you to address it.

Part amicably and celebrate contributions. Everyone is watching how the situation is being handled. It's okay to let people go if it's not working, but always treat them with dignity and respect, even on the way out.

Okay, now let's get down to what really matters. In our efforts to get the most out of employees we too often make a common mistake: We spend too much time worrying about poor performers and not enough time focusing on the best and the brightest. The real secret to making the biggest impact rests in investing in your best performers and ensuring they become even better.

Unfortunately, that rarely happens. Instead, the best players are viewed as so good that they are often left on their own. We have to think about it differently. If someone is tremendously good, you should ask, *What can I do to make them even better?* If someone is an A student, you must explore what you can do to make them an A+ student. The recipe for greatness is generally not found by taking a C student and making him or her a B student.

As the adage goes, "If you want something done, ask a busy person." I've seen this attributed to both Benjamin Franklin and Lucille Ball, but I especially like how my friend and former IBM boss, John Frandsen extended it: "Find a busy person and try to break them."

Go find your best people, inspire them, and ask more of them. What you will receive in return will astound you, and it is what will ensure your company's success today and tomorrow.

All the best,

Maynard

WHEN YOU NEED TO OWN BAD NEWS

Dear Founder,

You have good news and you're eager to share it. Don't.

Instead, let the person or team that accomplished this feat deliver the news. Then, you can add your thoughts—and kudos—on top. Everyone should have a chance to shine. (One disclaimer: If this information is going to the board, review it first, and use your judgement to decide who should send it. For example, if it is likely to generate follow-up questions you may want it to come from you.)

What about bad news? Do you have the folks you believe are responsible for something going wrong deliver a negative update? Here, the answer is a firm "no way." Don't ask them to deliver the news, and if they want to, don't let them.

When I was at eBay, any time there was a technology issue, it was up to me to call Meg Whitman personally. Since this was eBay in 1999, I had to call her in the middle of the night all the time. Meg's husband is a neurosurgeon and he always answered the phone, expecting it to be a patient with an emergency. I would say, "No one's dying, just my site, can I talk to Meg?" I knew that she wouldn't appreciate such a call from anyone else; it had to be me who told her what was happening, and I had to show that I was working with my teams to figure out the next step. Yet when it came to communicating what was happening to the board, that was Meg's job, not mine.

Recently I was reminded of this when one of the companies in WIN's portfolio missed its booking targets by around 40%. The company had previously signaled it would be short on the quarter, but not that short. Their head of sales sent out a note to the board taking responsibility. I respected this desire to take responsibility, but the note should have come from the CEO. That would have demonstrated that the whole company was on top of the problem, and working hard to fix it.

As a CEO, it's your responsibility to take ownership of delivering bad news. Don't ever distance yourself from it. You must also put context around it, explaining what it means. For example, you can't just say, "We missed the quarter" without detailing why it happened and how you'll make up for it. Your goal is to leave the recipient thinking, *Okay, thanks for the update,* as opposed to worrying about what they have to do now. Most board members react to bad news with action; it's up to you to give them enough information about how you're going to improve your issues, so they leave you alone to focus on fixing things.

No matter who's telling bad news, there needs to be good news sprinkled in with it. Your job isn't over just because you told the truth. You can't just ask people to absorb bad news constantly—that's not a recipe for greatness, let alone longevity! You should find a way to highlight progress, deliver some positive news, and leave people feeling optimistic.

My twelve-steps to consider implementing when you have to impart bad news:

1. Bad news doesn't get better with age; so don't wait (see the "When you have a crisis" letter).
2. Stay calm and focused.
3. Determine how bad it is.
4. Figure out who needs to know.
5. If it's seriously bad, consult with your lawyers and advisers and listen to them.
6. Decide what to disclose. (Don't overreact, and don't underreact!)
7. Make sure the information comes from you.
8. Tell the truth, admit the situation, and own up to the seriousness of it.
9. Share what you are doing to resolve the issue and move ahead.

10. Set expectations for what progress will look like.
11. Don't expect anyone to be happy with very bad news.
12. Ask for help, and ask those receiving the bad news what else you can be doing.

Delivering bad news isn't fun; I always dreaded making emergency calls or writing negative update emails to Meg. However, that pain forced me to figure out what we could do, so I could make that call or write that note less often. And we did. We never stopped communicating with Meg, but as the team got stronger and we got better, I delivered fewer bad updates, and the team started sending their own notes with good news. I wish the same for you.

All the best,

Maynard

WHEN YOU NEED TO SET THE TONE FOR APPROPRIATE BEHAVIOR

Dear Founder,

It's important to set the right tone for your company from its very earliest days. Most important: Treat everyone with dignity and respect, always.

You usually know the right way to behave, but if you find yourself in an uncertain situation, picture whatever you are doing showing up on the front page of *The New York Times.* How would you feel about that? Better yet, how would you feel about your mother reading it? (Those were scenarios that Meg Whitman used to pose to us at eBay.) At Bain, they call it the "Sunshine Test" (as in, how would you feel if this were exposed in broad daylight?).

There's been a rash of news lately about investors, CEOs, and people in leadership positions behaving badly. We're all learning more and more about the sexual harassment problems in Silicon Valley, in the entertainment industry, the media, government, and more.

I'm thrilled that people are speaking up, because we need more awareness and visibility on this issue to end these ugly episodes. However, we can't just wait for whistle-blowers. Leaders play the most significant role in ending these problems. They must examine how they can prevent abuse from happening and take a critical look at their own behaviors.

If you have not yet set the right tone, now is the time:

- Be maniacally clear about what behavior is expected in your workplace. Have guidelines on what is and isn't acceptable and guidelines on how you hold people accountable.
- Do not promote a monoculture, such as a "bro culture"—this is antiquated and dangerous. Have a workplace that

supports and celebrates diversity and makes everyone feel comfortable.

- Celebrating teams and wins is a good thing. Having validations and rewards for people is important. Yet leaders must remember their leadership roles, even when outside of the office. They can never lose control or go over the top. I know of a company that has a holiday party tradition where the CEO matches the employees "shot for shot." That's stupid on his part. Regardless of how smart or well-behaved you normally are, alcohol (and other substances) alters your judgment and impacts your inhibitions.
- Understand, flat out, it is never okay to apply pressure in an unwelcome way on anybody. Additionally, you must always be aware of your position before getting romantically involved. Do not ever become romantically involved with a subordinate. Remember: the greater responsibility and authority you have at the company, the less freedom you have in this regard.
- Never do anything unethical or illegal. Enough said.
- Understand that perception is reality. We live in a world of extreme transparency and winnowed privacy. There are cameras everywhere. Anything can be videoed. Bad behavior is likely to be captured and published. Do not put yourself in any inappropriate or compromising situation. If you are in a position of power, it does not matter if you didn't "do" anything. Even the appearance of doing something will be harmful.
- Remember to stay human. It's easy to see when something is over the line and wrong, but there are more gray and nuanced issues.

  - Is it ever okay to hug someone at work? I think so—as long as it is welcome.

- What about saying, "you guys"? I used to say that all the time and I would say it meaning to encompass everyone. Now, that feels wrong and I'm working on migrating to a different term, like "team" or "people" or "y'all." (I am from Florida).
- Asking someone out for a drink alone? (Probably not okay if they work for you.)

Leaders are held to higher standards. The higher you go, the more obligated you are to set an example. Do the right thing.

All the best,

Maynard

5
Personal Challenges of Leadership

WHEN YOU ARE OVERWHELMED

Dear Founder,

I'm sorry you're feeling overwhelmed. Unfortunately, this is a normal feeling for most of us. *The important thing is to realize that this is a momentary state.* By shifting into action, you can get rid of this uncomfortable feeling.

A couple of personal stories from the mundane to the very strategic:

Just a few weeks ago, I had a very early start to the morning as I had a two-hour commute to San Francisco for an 8 a.m. meeting. I got up extra early, dressed, and rushed down to my office to do a few critical emails before taking off. My email was locked up and as I attempted to refresh, it was not recognizing the correct password. I had a serious head cold and was feeling bad. *Why is this happening to me?* I thought. I took some deep breaths, rebooted my computer, and got everything back to normal. Sometimes, in stressful times, even the smallest issues can seem insurmountable—but when you take a step out of the moment and implement the action necessary to solve it, you find that these issues are never impossible and are not worth a fraction of the grief they caused.

Last week, I was executing on a long-planned surprise birthday party for my wife in Jackson Hole, Wyoming. We had family and friends flying in from all over to help celebrate. My family had all arrived by 5 p.m. and we were heading to dinner at 7 p.m. where all our friends would also surprise my wife. At the same time, we were in the middle of negotiations at Salesforce to buy Demandware and I was heading the M&A committee. I thought I had everything well-managed as we had a 2 p.m. call for the Salesforce board. Plenty of time to get everything under control. But then, the company asked for more time to consider the deal. We got a call at 5:30 p.m. asking to have an additional board call at 6 p.m. We were twenty-five minutes away from the restaurant where the party would take place. *Why was this happening to me?* I explained the situation to my family (they're used to these "bomb-ins" by now) and gave a precautionary heads-up to the person running the party. We drilled down on what was necessary with the board, and managed to keep the board call focused to accomplish the necessary discussion. We got to the party on time and the surprise went off without a hitch. However, I was definitely feeling stressed and overwhelmed, and it certainly wreaked havoc on my blood pressure!

The whole Yahoo! journey, which I can't really talk about, has had lots of moments where being overwhelmed was a very real possibility (e.g., activist shareholders, core business not turning around fast enough, damaging external press, etc.). The one thing that kept everyone sane is that the board was very aligned around selling the company. It was the shift to action—rather than focusing on all the negative possibilities—that removed much of the feeling of being overwhelmed.

In most cases, the first reaction to something that is frustrating is to focus on how this is not a great situation and to question, *Why is it happening to me?* This kind of thinking, while natural, is not conducive to getting the situation solved. I wrote another letter about what to do if you are in a crisis, but I'll share the CliffsNotes version here:

Start taking action and focus your energy on resolution.

In almost all situations where you feel overwhelmed, follow this five-step plan:

1. Slow down.
2. Ask questions.
3. Get your bearings.
4. Develop a plan that you believe in.
5. Start taking proactive actions.

Recognizing that feeling overwhelmed is an emotional state, and that it can be overcome through a measured, practiced approach, has been one of the skills I've benefited from the most over my career (I've had several jobs that have had lots of crises and drama in them—I'm not sure why I'm so lucky). For more on this topic, David Rock's book *Your Brain at Work* gives a fantastic overview of the cognitive limits of the brain.

Once I realize that I am feeling overwhelmed, I don't need to actually fix everything to get rid of the overwhelmed feeling; I just need a plan that I believe in and that I can start executing. Things that have worked for me:

- **I proactively manage my calendar and my to-dos.** Anticipate as much as possible. Ask yourself: What's likely to interrupt the most important things? Develop ways to absorb the bomb-ins.
- **I don't expect perfection on all of my to-dos, but I do expect to accomplish the most important things.** I've always found that the worry about how long something will take to get done is far worse than the actual time it usually takes to do it. So, as Nike says, "Just do it."
- **I build in time every week for reflection and ensure that I'm grounded on what matters most.** All of us are busy, but we must not confuse action with traction.
- **I try very hard to not be a bottleneck.** (See the letter called "When you need to improve execution.")

We're all faced with feeling overwhelmed at times, but it's not becoming for a CEO to appear overwhelmed. Remember, you're a leader and people will take their cues on how to handle a situation from you. You will generally have information ahead of most others in the company. If you find you're overwhelmed, take the time to process this privately so that public communication to employees and others can be done professionally and proactively.

The most important thing to do when you do become overwhelmed is to stay calm, and recognize that the best thing to do to conquer this sensation is to shift into taking action and executing on a well-thought-out plan.

All the best,

Maynard

WHEN YOU HAVE TO FACE THAT YOUR STARTUP IS FAILING

Dear Founder,

I am so sorry that you have found a need for this letter.

Please understand that you are not alone. From a hiring misstep, to a botched product launch, to a company that never gains traction: startup founders have to deal with all kinds of failure. Yet what really matters is *how* we deal with it. I've seen failure addressed in two very different ways:

1. Rationalization

As an investor, I often hear a lot of reasons from founders for their issues: "The market wasn't ready," "The product wasn't ready," "We were burning though cash too quickly." Well, *who* chose the market? *Who* developed the product? *Who* spent the cash? When it comes to dealing with failure, recovering from failure, and learning from failure, it's important to take responsibility for any missteps. That's the only way to ensure that they won't be repeated.

2. Responsibility

When things go wrong, I am always looking to see whether or not the founders own the outcome and the mistakes that led to the outcome, and I appreciate and give credit to people who are self-aware and learn from their errors. At the same time, it's important to be a bit wary, as some people may take responsibility as lip service, rather than feel it viscerally.

What are you supposed to do? A few thoughts on how to fail with grace and dignity:

Get out of the gray zone. Being in the murky area where you keep spending money and are "hoping" for a turnaround is a bad place to be. You need to know: Is this right or not? If the idea isn't good enough or big enough, determine if there is a pivot to be made. What do you need to do to restructure? What do you have to do differently? We recently had one of our portfolio companies pivot and replace the CEO—changes that saved the company. However, changing the CEO is not a panacea. In rare cases, the founder comes back to save the day like Steve Jobs did at Apple or Michael Dell did at Dell.

Know when to let go. If the idea is never going to make it, determine how to sell the technology and the talent and return some capital to investors. One of our portfolio companies arranged a talent acquisition to Google. In finding a home for their team members, the founders took care of their engineers and returned all the cash they raised to investors.

Treat people the way you want to be treated. As you would with any job, leave on good terms. By treating everyone with respect, you give people another opportunity to remember you in a positive light. You want people to feel as if you treated them as well as possible even though the company did not reach its full potential. It is very likely that you will want do another startup, and how you handle your failures now will set a precedent for how likely you will be to obtain funding for your future endeavors. If you flame out, it will be much harder for anyone to support you next time. Specifically:

- **Communicate early.** Surprises are bad things, especially when all the money is gone. People should know the company is in trouble before it folds. Investors might be able to help get the company on the right path. Give them the opportunity.
- **Take care of your customers.** Don't crash and burn and leave them with nothing. If you have customers on your service, educate them on places to migrate and give them a

date for the end of life of the service. (Try to keep it running for ninety days or more after you notify them.)

- **Be generous with your employees.** Make sure they have other jobs. I believe some severance is in order. There are some tough calls here about who gets what, and at what expense to investors, and there are no hard and fast rules. The decisions you make will be very situational and depend on team performance among other things. The operative word in this calculus is *fairness*.

Turn your focus to, "Now what?" Determine if you have the stomach to start a company again. Do you have the passion and enthusiasm to go after it again, or do you want to pursue a safer route, with more predictable economics? Take the opportunity to step back and reflect: What really went wrong? What have you learned about yourself that you didn't know before? Are you ready to do it all again?

Part of entrepreneurship is failing. Don't feel horrible about it. Don't lose your drive to change the world and make a difference.

Remember, true innovation rests on trying, failing, and trying again. Thomas Edison discovered hundreds of ways not to build the lightbulb before he found a way to make it something we can't live without. Babe Ruth held a record for strikeouts—not just home runs. And, Henry Ford had two car companies fail before he created the one that revolutionized modern production. The world needs more entrepreneurs who are bold enough to think of new ideas and brave enough to pursue them.

All the best,

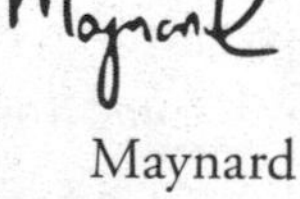

Maynard

WHEN YOU NEED INSPIRATION

Dear Founder,

You're needing some inspiration right now. Maybe you're looking for a great idea, or perhaps you need to find another way to solve a gnarly problem.

Where does inspiration come from? How do you get it? I think there are many people far more qualified than I am to talk about inspiration and its genesis. And there are certainly some great resources, including the book *Creative Confidence* by IDEO's David and Tom Kelley, which talks about the value of having a beginner's mind, or author Elizabeth Gilbert's TED Talk on where genius comes from.

Everyone sources inspiration differently. Sometimes it's the result of a eureka moment, but more often it's the result of hard work, serendipity, and having an open mind—seeing opportunities where others saw constraints (or maybe even nothing at all). Pierre Omidyar was just hacking around when he stumbled on the idea for eBay. Marc Benioff had the idea for Salesforce while on sabbatical from Oracle and swimming with dolphins in Hawaii. And he had the inspiration to incorporate philanthropy into the business from leaders he admired, including Amma (the hugging saint) and Colin Powell. President Kennedy expanded the US space program and set an ambitious goal to put a man on the moon because the Russians had leapt ahead of the United States in the space race with Sputnik, and he was inspired to redefine what the finish line should be.

For me, inspiration often starts with frustration. It begins with what seems like intractable problems—and then an unwillingness to accept that there are not any answers. I keep these intractable problems in my head and keep a lookout for answers or insights that can come from anywhere. Let me give you a couple of examples from my experience.

When I was at eBay, we had a very thorny search problem. Search experts like Google and Yahoo! were unwilling to help solve our problem. We did find a vendor we were convinced could fix it, but after a year of attempting to make it work, the team came to me and said it wouldn't work. Our search capability was degrading daily and it was costing us a fortune. The team didn't know what to do. I didn't know what to do. I called together our best and brightest. I didn't have an exact agenda or assignments to dole out, but I explained the entire situation: "Here's the intractable problem. I know we can fix it and here's what it all looks like when we're done. I have money, please tell me what else you need and I will make it happen." That ignited something. The team delivered a radically better and cheaper solution in six months or so.

Believe it or not, the inspiration for WIN also stemmed from an intractable problem—in this case, a personal one. My wife and I had agreed that I would not "run" anything once I stepped down as the LiveOps CEO. I had also committed that to her that I would only run LiveOps for five years. I didn't want to retire. I knew that I still had a lot to contribute, but because of my promise to her, I couldn't do it in a traditional way. I was pretty stuck.

One Sunday night while my wife was out of town, I agreed to go to an FCC chairman dinner in San Francisco on a Sunday night. While there, Mitch Kapor, a Silicon Valley legend and the entrepreneur who started Lotus, and I started talking about what we were working on and he invited me to come see him soon. On the day of our scheduled meeting, I got in the car wondering whether this would be a wise use of my time, but I had committed so I went. Once there, Mitch shared with me what he was doing with Kapor Enterprises. I walked away from that meeting realizing that *I* got to choose how I wanted to spend my time going forward. Instead of hoping to be selected to someone else's team, I could create my own. Within weeks, I built the foundation for WIN. It's been the right solution to my career conundrum and it's also been very fulfilling.

Even the idea for Everwise grew out of a problem. I was working on my book and bothered by the limits of the publishing world. It took so long for the book to come out, and the publisher also rebuffed my ideas to develop a companion application. I walked away very irritated. But then I took that annoyance and used it to inspire something else. I challenged myself: "I bet I can start a whole company before the book comes out." The idea for Everwise came to me—mentoring was on my mind and was a chapter in the book—and I knew the world needed a service to help match and manage mentors and mentees. We did get it started before the book came out, and now it's much more than a fun challenge, it's a real company.

WIN is more fun and more challenging than I originally had imagined, but I knew after a few years that there was more we should be doing. We needed to engage the network in a whole new way to unlock more of its power. Instead of just funding great new companies, we decided to create great new ones from scratch. And so I stumbled on another problem—and a solution. WIN Labs is still a baby, but I know it will become an interesting new capability we'll bring to the world.

Even if you do not have the answers you need right now, I promise you that your solutions are all out there. You just need to acknowledge that you have a sticky issue, commit to solving it, and go about your journey with an air of wonder and an understanding that magic can and will happen.

You have to start with "how can I" instead of "I can't." Here's to your inspiration journey—may it be rich and rewarding!

All the best,

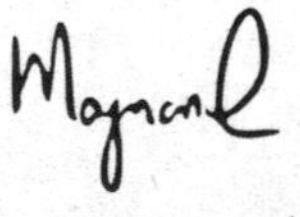

Maynard

WHEN YOU'RE DEALT BODY BLOWS

Dear Founder,

My sister recently sent me the obituary for Dr. George Diaz, our next-door neighbor from our childhood in Florida. Dr. Diaz was the dentist in town, and he was always there at the right moment in my life. He was available to perform emergency surgery on my fifth birthday when my dad's attempt to pull my loose tooth with a string tied to a door handle went very awry. He was at the ready when I chipped my tooth playing football with my brother. He was available when I knocked out my two front teeth after I flipped over my bicycle's handlebars delivering papers. "Do you still have the teeth?" he asked. I did—and he put them back.

Dr. Diaz was a good soul, and thinking about him got me thinking about resilience. He saw some of my earliest body blows, and maybe in part because of him, I knew that you had to pick yourself (and your teeth) up, recover, and move on to the next adventure.

I often talk about body blows—we all receive them. And, as a founder—one of the hardest jobs in the world—you'll face your fair share of knocks. However, what's important is not that you have these blows, or how big they are, but instead it's how you deal with them and what you learn from them.

In my career, and in my life, I've found that what derails one person can barely put a dent in another.

I recently faced one of my worst body blows, when some terrible news from several years ago emerged about one of the companies I'm involved with. It was so big it would take your breath away. But you can only let that happen for a short period of time, or you're admitting defeat! When something bad happens, you have two choices: you can curl up in the covers and stay in bed, or you can pick yourself up and achieve what you set out to do.

That's exactly what I saw happen recently when the CEO of one of our breakout companies handled a body blow. A top executive—whom he had landed after a yearlong search—quit unexpectedly after just six months on the job. Instead of letting that derail him or the company, he immediately got back on his feet and started interviewing great candidates.

That was the right approach—and the only approach. Of course it can be easier said than done. You always have to pick yourself up, but how?

When you are hit with something painful, it hurts. First, embrace how it feels. Acknowledge the pain. Understand that this experience, while difficult in the moment, will ultimately make you stronger. I always think about the biblical verse I first read a long time ago from James: "When troubles of any kind come your way, consider it an opportunity for great joy. For you know that when your faith is tested, your endurance has a chance to grow."

Go through the healing. Do what you have to do to fix the problem—whether it's seeing the dentist for some knocked-out teeth, speaking with someone about your loss, or taking the time you need to recover from an injury.

Don't become callous. Some people can deal with anything and lose their humanity after experiencing losses. They become hard, or they become selfish. Take the learnings from the body blows with sensitivity and care. Gain wisdom and understanding, not an edge. Let this setback help you empathize with more people.

Understand that this hit cannot keep you from going back. How quickly you can recover is important. You must get back into the ring—you cannot be afraid to be put at risk again. Bad things happen, but if you let them derail you, they win.

Rebuild your muscles. And, increase your flexibility to handle things differently next time.

Get fired up. Unfortunately you've just been delivered a significant body blow. I'm sorry about that, but now you must get back up—there's too much good work that needs to be done to let yourself wallow in self-pity.

Resilience is not just about intestinal fortitude and grit. Resilience also encapsulates potential. Every time you get close to your potential, it expands. Everyone—and especially leaders and top executives—needs to possess that kind of resilience. Without it, you stay in your safe zone. That's not where excellence happens. It's where average and mediocre happens.

Never stop teaching yourself how to handle more and get good at picking yourself up. This is what leadership and growth is all about.

All the best,

Maynard

WHEN YOU NEED TO PUT THE COMPANY'S NEEDS AHEAD OF YOUR OWN

Dear Founder,

You may be grappling with one of the hardest issues any leader faces—when do you put the company's needs above your own?

Being the CEO of a company sounds like a great job—until you actually have to perform the work and you quickly find that this work must come before your own personal desires. You'll find that the chief leadership role requires you to put the entity's mission ahead of your own goals. Sometimes, it's a huge wake-up call.

At least it was for me. When I became a manager at IBM, I realized how much more responsibility I had than when I was an individual contributor. Comments that I used to make in jest were interpreted with fear (e.g., "Is my job in jeopardy?"). I also realized that employees expected me to fix their concerns about the department. This was my first experience understanding the broader role of a leader versus an individual team member, which is what I had been in the past.

As my career progressed, I landed new jobs and kept getting excited about gaining bigger and bigger roles, including CIO jobs, a COO role, and a CEO role. I took on board roles and even served as chairman a few times. There were countless times when I had to do something for the good of the entity at a personal sacrifice to myself. As a matter of course, I would often take less compensation for myself to ensure that my star employees could receive more. I canceled family vacations, including turning around one time on the way to an airport. I once was asked to spend almost half a year in China away from my home and family to help turn around eBay. This "opportunity" occurred during my son's final year in high school and in the middle of building our dream home. Meg Whitman asked me to grade, on a scale of 1 to 10 (with 10 being the highest), my enthusiasm for the assignment. I answered honestly, "a '1' or a '2.'" I was told, "You're going anyway." And so, I went. I did my best to put my heart and soul into fixing things at the company, but it came at a big family cost. (In hindsight, this sacrifice was worth it, but in the moment I was not so certain—neither was my family.)

A year later, when my daughter was about to enter her senior year in high school, I was asked to transfer to Europe to run Skype. This time I put my family first, but also knew that decision meant it was time for me to leave eBay. It's not that eBay required that I resign; it's that I realized that I was unwilling to put the mission above my personal desires, which felt wrong as the number two person at the company. I have never regretted the decision not to move and the subsequent decision to leave; it was the right call because of what I was willing to give at the time.

There are all sorts of leaders, from command-and-control leaders who bark orders and expect everyone to toe the line, to inspirational servant leaders who put the entity's needs above their own. The most inspiring CEOs are committed to changing the world, and they are able to do so by putting the destiny of the company ahead of their own ego or needs. (Where it gets really tricky is being able to simultaneously take care of all the entities they are part of—their company, their family, their team.)

Your leadership style is personal, so don't let anyone else decide how you want to deploy the CEO role at your company. CEOs approach their role in different ways. Yet in order to determine if they still deserve the role, every great CEO needs to examine their performance and periodically ask themselves:

- Am I driving/leading the company forward, or am I holding it back?
- What unique contributions am I making to the success and future of the company? Would I rehire myself as CEO? Why?

- Am I getting managed into compliance by the team? Or am I challenging the team to get to previously unimagined capabilities?
- When I do challenge the team and then later look back with hindsight, was pushing them the right thing to do, or did it cause unnecessary churn and a failure to reach the desired result? Why?

Sometimes, when you're tired or overwhelmed, you need to harden your resolve and dig deeper. I have a lot of belief in founders and their willingness and commitment to do the unthinkable. However, if you no longer have the burning desire to take on the challenges and responsibilities that come with the top job, you may need to put the company's success ahead of your own. And, that may mean stepping aside.

Being a leader is hard work and it requires tons of personal sacrifice. You have to manage your employees, your customers, and your board and investors. The founder of the private equity firm TPG once compared being a CEO to playing three-dimensional chess. It's insanely difficult.

You have the toughest and the coolest job on the planet. I wish you strength.

All the best,

Maynard

WHEN YOU'RE CONFUSING HUBRIS WITH BOLDNESS

Dear Founder,

You've founded a company—essentially, you've created something from nothing. That's alchemy. As a founder, you have an outsized desire for greatness for your company. That's bold. You might also think you have ideas or talents no one else has ever had. That's hubris.

And that's (mostly) okay. The fact is you have to possess that kind of belief to do something that's new, different, and world class. However, you also need to back up what you say. Your "say-to-do" ratio needs to be high. After all, your vision doesn't matter if it doesn't become a reality. In other words, you need to deliver.

All of this makes common sense, but the fact is there's a fine line between confidence and cockiness. We've all experienced how some people can infect you with their enthusiasm, while others can infuriate you with their arrogance—and we all know the impression it imparts is anything but subtle.

At WIN, we spend a lot of time meeting with entrepreneurs, and the bold versus hubris conversation comes up a lot. What shows boldness? I always appreciate hearing why someone believes their idea and approach is a winning one. Of course everybody that comes in thinks they have a winning strategy, but when someone truly has conviction, it shows. How? It's when someone can crisply articulate the vision, the value proposition, the market, and the potential. They have clarity on what their next steps are and what will be done with the money. Rather than downplay competitors as dumb or naïve, they explain what the strengths of each are, and why those strengths will make it difficult for them to outcompete this new startup.

Yet here's the one thing that signals a bold attitude that might be more counterintuitive: being secure enough to identify the parade of horrible things that can go wrong. I'm impressed with someone who says, "We don't have it all figured out yet" or "It's early but here's what we've seen so far." No business plan or model is ever bulletproof, and I appreciate the entrepreneurs who highlight the unknowns. Being upfront about all of the possibilities, good and bad, shows that the entrepreneur is thoughtful, rational, and disciplined. It also shows that they are honest and recognize the need to learn.

(Note: You should still know *some* things for certain. For example, if you're raising money, you should have already talked with potential users or customers; you should understand competitors, etc.)

Hubris, on the other hand, is dangerous. Sometimes we uncover it when a founder says that they have a hot, oversubscribed round, and it's actually a ploy to make investors move artificially fast, when no one has committed. While there are legitimate speedy rounds that require fast decisions, no one appreciates being misled. Other signals that start to signal hubris for us include not preparing or sharing a deck in advance, grandiose answers for how big the market is, poor answers for how they will monetize their business, and aggressive and difficult-to-believe projections. We love extraordinary enthusiasm and passion, but as long as it comes with corresponding evidence in the team, market, or product to warrant such exuberance.

Overall, the biggest difference between boldness and hubris, though, has to do with listening. Bold entrepreneurs are thoughtful and good listeners. They may not necessarily implement our advice (and that's okay), but we want to see that they value and consider outside input.

Unfortunately, it's common for entrepreneurs—once they've achieved some success—to fall victim to thinking they have it all figured out. I've noticed a funny paradox that happens as you rise in your career. When you start out, you sometimes have to be loud to simply break through the noise; later, once you've "made it," everyone listens and agrees, even when maybe they shouldn't. Here are some ways to keep your bold attitude in the forefront and keep the hubris at bay:

- **Show vulnerability to build trust.** In the past, I remember thinking that revealing any vulnerability would be a sign of weakness. I was so worried when I got hearing aids in my forties, and I thought that my career would be over. How wrong was I about that! It's counterintuitive, but I found that the more vulnerabilities I shared, the more grace I received. As an executive, you feel pressure to be perfect, but the more human you are, the more you are genuine and authentic, and the more people relate to you and support you. (My hearing aids turned out to be a gift—when people rambled on too long in meetings, I'd simply make a joke of turning down the hearing aids, and everyone quickly got the message.)
- **Own the mistakes.** Every pro-football player fumbles. What matters is that you jump on the ball. When you make a mistake, admit it as quickly as possible. Apologize and explain it, fix it, and move on. I learned this lesson at eBay when I had to implement a hiring shutdown. It was necessary for the business, and it was effective, but we did it in an inelegant way that left managers feeling disempowered, out of the loop, and very bitter. We realized our mistake and apologized at a meeting. We received a nice round of applause for that, and I learned how to do better by being more inclusive of everyone the next time. As a leader, remember that your example is the lead your employees will follow. (Of course, you shouldn't make a habit of making mistakes—routine issues are a quick way to lose credibility.)
- **Your critics are your greatest mentors.** Sure, it sounds great to have everyone rally around you and think you are fabulous—until you recall the tale of "The Emperor's New Clothes." When you strip away the good feelings that come

with people saying nice things about your every move, you realize you don't just want "yes people" around you. "Yes people," the people who support you and never question you, will not help you get any better. Instead of only having people who are drinking your own Kool-Aid, you need to have people around you who are honest and critical. They may annoy you, but they will help you stay true to what you're good at, and help you get better at what you haven't yet mastered. It's hard to do this, so put policies in place that help. At WIN, my team makes recommendations for investments, and I have to be supportive of every company we invest in. Historically, having such a process has led to better decision-making for us, but in the rare cases when my team feels strongly about a company and I disagree, I am willing to hear their perspectives and invest. And when I'm excited and the team strongly disagrees, we will discuss until we reach a conclusion we're all happy with.

- **Stay humble and don't read your own press clippings!** As you succeed—which we hope you do—you will have to work harder to be your own biggest critic. Of course you have to believe in yourself, and be proud of what you've accomplished—but only feel that for two seconds. There is strong evidence that decision-making can be directly influenced by leaders' public perception. Recent great press can lead to grandiose, reckless decisions, and recent bad press can lead to dangerously meek moves (for more on this interesting phenomenon, check out *Decisive* by Chip and Dan Heath). To stay centered, I try to remember where I came from, and recall the breaks, privileges, and good fortune that have helped me along my path. Pay attention to that, thank the people who helped you, and pay it forward by helping others the way people have helped you.

Once you've made it, you're expected to know all of the answers and have no doubts. That's so unrealistic. No one's perfect—and there's no milestone (e.g., becoming CEO, raising a round, going public, etc.) that suddenly changes that.

With experience, you learn that being the best you can be doesn't mean doing everything right, it means constantly striving to be better. You also learn that the behavior and aggressive stance that was essential to your success early in your career can derail your success in the next part of your career. So, temper the hubris and tame the arrogance, but never stop being brave and bold.

All the best,

Maynard

WHEN YOU'RE ACCUSED OF WORKING TOO MUCH

Dear Founder,

Work-life balance? As I have often said in response to this question: "Are you friggin' kidding me?"

It is not that work-life balance is not important—it is—it's just that if you're a founder, you've *already* decided that work will take most of your focus for the next several years. I have yet to be pitched by a founder who said having great work-life balance was a prerequisite. I have funded a lot of entrepreneurs who were working long hours to make a difference. I'll never forget how the founders of Grubwithus, one of the companies in our portfolio (now known as GOAT), slept in a car when they were trying to raise seed funding. That said a lot to me about their focus on the company and the sacrifices they were willing to make to ensure it would be successful. Of course, not every founder has the freedom to take those kinds of risks—and that's okay, too.

Building a transformative company requires heroics from many people, and particularly from the founders. In starting a company, the unfortunate reality is that there's no such thing as balance. Taking an idea to greatness requires extreme—Herculean—efforts.

We all know that starting a company is not for the faint of heart. Most startups fail. In the early stages of a startup, you have to be maniacally focused. Startup life is not—and should not be—for everyone. If you want to self-fund your company, you can do whatever you want. However, if you want to take outside money, investors will expect total commitment, as that's what it takes to break out of the morass. If you want to do something game changing, if you want to grow a thousand times bigger, if you want to transform an industry or change the world, there are likely to be difficult trade-offs.

Sometimes these trade-offs will be worth the cost, and other times they won't be. If they are not, don't commit to doing your job halfway. Many years ago, I was recruited to be the number two person at a hot startup. The job was supposed to be in the Bay Area, but then the new CEO, a former Microsoft exec, wanted to relocate the business to Seattle. My wife had zero interest in leaving Silicon Valley for Seattle. She didn't want to hold me back, though, saying I could commute there and come home on the weekends. "It's a startup," I said. "There are no weekends." (She was familiar with this kind of work schedule; she still enjoys telling people how when I was at Thomas-Conrad when it was a startup in Austin I once called in sick—on a Sunday.) Knowing the amount of time the new post would require, I politely declined the Seattle-based job and went to a company that was in a different phase and allowed me to be with my family.

While building a startup requires many demands and sacrifices, founders must also be mindful of their family situation and take what's best for their loved ones into careful and constant consideration. Family must not be left behind for the needs of a company. A business succeeding at the expense of family is a failure. If you achieve wild success, but have lost your spouse and your children, what's the point?

And, a business can never succeed without the support and understanding of a founder's loved ones. At the start of founding a company, founders should ensure that their partners are fully aware and bought into the challenge. Before starting your business, consider talking to other people—founders and their spouses—about what the real sacrifices are. At the same time, founders need to know when to be there for family regardless of work.

As always, communication on this issue with your loved ones is key. That doesn't mean that your partner will always understand or that there won't be tension. There will not always be harmony, but you should always communicate what you are doing and why it's important. There are certain times, an IPO road show for example, where balance will become even more out of whack and it's best to highlight what will happen in advance. Companies should also try to bring significant others into the fold and make them feel welcome, which will not eliminate the burden of those left at home, but it will help them to better understand what's happening and why it's necessary.

Choosing between work and family demands can ignite hard decisions, but there are right decisions to be made and you can figure out this balancing act. Sometimes it's painfully obvious. When my daughter was a baby, she contracted *E. coli* and was gravely ill. She was in intensive care for eight weeks and we weren't sure she was going to make it. My wife, Irene, took a leave of absence from work. I worked part-time.

Other times, you need a framework to help you with the day-to-day conundrums. Brad Smith, the CEO of Intuit who spoke at a WIN Summit, articulated this constant dilemma very well. He describes two categories of moments in life: "rubber ball moments" and "crystal ball moments." He said of the rubber ball moments, if you drop them, they'll bounce and come back. With the crystal ball moments, if you let them drop, they shatter and they never come back. "Our key in life is to make sure we know which is which," Brad said.

He offered examples in his own life with his two daughters. One is a dancer who had fifteen dance recitals last year. She wanted him at every one, but he couldn't deliver on that. "I knew if I let one dance recital drop it would bounce and next week I'd be at another one. She would be hurt, but it wouldn't be forever," he said. Brad defined a crystal ball moment as high school graduation. That happens one time. If dropped, it shatters forever. "I never ever prioritize work over a crystal moment, but I have to make trade-offs at times when it's rubber. I'm very *very* clear about which those moments are," Brad explained.

Technology, and the constant connectivity it offers, has made many of the daily choices both easier and harder. In a world that's connected 24/7, in which we check email after dinner (and sometimes during dinner), and we can work from home when the kids are off from school, there's no longer such a thing as on-hours and off-hours. Our work and personal lives often collide, and they will only continue to do so.

The best way to make it all work is not to silo off these distinct parts, but to weave them together into a custom tapestry. If you do that, and if you are truly doing what you love, it trumps the desire for balance and achieves something better, something magical.

All the best,

Maynard

WHEN YOU SELF-IMPOSE LIMITS

Dear Founder,

> *"I can't take a risk because I have a mortgage to pay."*
> *"I can't accept my dream job because I'd have to move."*
> *"I can't work after-hours because my spouse would be mad at me."*

I hear these statements—these self-imposed limits—every day. As humans, we often have too pessimistic a view on what is possible, and we let the world convince us we can't do something, instead of thinking, *How can I?*

Well, most of the time we are wrong. Remember, common sense once *knew* the world was flat, and that travel by horse was the fastest speed man could go. When I was younger, I wholeheartedly believed that I was going to die at age forty-seven because my dad did.

Wrong, wrong, wrong.

When you create limits that don't really exist, you are justifying where you are. And where you are is never as great as where you *could* be. By setting limits you're effectively deciding not to reach for more. Therefore, you must push through the limits that you're imposing on yourself.

But how?

Take a pause. Find out where the limits stem from and why you're reinforcing them. Oftentimes, we have our own big beliefs that we never question. When my parents first married, my father wanted to become a real estate appraiser. However, this job required special training and certification and he thought that being married and having kids would make it too difficult. My mom helped him see that this goal and family life weren't incompatible. "Why set limits?" she asked. "We can do this." They moved to Gainesville, Florida, he enrolled in a program, and he earned his certification.

Recognize that you are holding yourself back. Yes, the world tries to hold us back at times, but the most constraining limits you have are the ones you put on yourself. It's easy to blame society, the government, the economy, your health, or your family—and all of these can be challenging or completely debilitating—but generally we put more limits on ourselves than any outside force ever can. Instead of blaming others for setbacks, accept accountability and understand that you are the one who is responsible for chasing—and catching—your dreams.

Make choices carefully. Every choice comes with trade-offs; it's up to you to decide if they're worth it. Once I started advancing in my career, I knew that I didn't have the educational chops that my peers had. That made me feel inferior in some ways, and at one point, when I was already a CIO, I thought about going to back to school to get an MBA. At the time, I was the sole provider for four kids, so this decision carried tremendous consequences for my family. I went to some friends and mentors for advice, and I learned a lot about decision-making—and about myself. My friend Andy Ludwick had a great career and a Harvard MBA, and his guidance surprised me. "Maynard, this would come at a huge opportunity cost, and you are in your prime earning years," he said. "Most people go back to school to learn how to do stuff you are already doing, and they go for the network, which you already have. This is not worth the cost for you." That was very freeing. I had always been ashamed to talk about my background for fear of being judged, which was why I wanted to go back to school. I wanted to compensate for what I thought I was lacking. The discussion with Andy made me realize that it was all in my head—I wasn't really lacking what I needed to know—and then I realized that my story also had value. My background and its lack of pedigree—once I leaned into it—turned out to be inspirational to others. It showed the opportunity we all have to achieve, regardless of where we come from.

Play out all of the options and know where they lead. When I was in my late twenties I was starting to get some traction in my career, but I was still exploring different paths and trying to see where they would take me. I loved watching people lead and knew I wanted to be a manager. I was enamored with the art of HR and coaching, but I was also very drawn to technology. I was working in security—even though I loved and longed for the managing people piece—but there were lots of opportunities in tech and I didn't hold myself back from participating. There were myriad of things people didn't want to do, including getting called into work in the middle of the night, or working weekends. I volunteered, because I was eager to prove myself, and had no illusions that any task was beneath me. I got my first management job, which I coveted and others didn't because it required working two Saturdays a month and doing payroll rather than managing professionals. A year into that role, I began to manage professional IT workers, and a year after that, IBM promoted me to a middle-management role. Instead of imposing limits on myself by declaring, "I won't work weekends" or "I only want to work on exciting things," I remained open to all options and saw them as paths to the potential I was chasing.

If there is a recipe for success, I believe that it is this: Get out of defense mode and go into wonder mode. Every time you hear yourself say, "I can't," dive in and ask, "Why? What are the reasons I can't?" Upon introspection, you might realize that many of the things you feel are holding you back, exist nowhere but in your head.

All of us possess a potential that is boundless. Every time you push against it, it expands. I can't wait to see how far you go.

All the best,

Maynard

WHEN THE WORLD TRIES TO MANAGE YOU

Dear Founder,

It happens every day. Instead of leaving you to chart your own course, the world steps in and tries to direct you to go a different way. Sometimes you already have a perfectly good plan mapped out, and this divergence is not entirely welcome. Yet that doesn't mean you can ignore it; you still have to deal with what's been thrown right in front of you.

Earlier in my career, when I was first a director in charge of IT, I had finally made it to the executive ranks, but still the world didn't see my future trajectory the way I did. I was reminded that I didn't come from an Ivy League school and that I was homegrown. I received feedback that I was a good "blue collar" executive—good for the engine room, but not for the boardroom.

Later this happened to me again when I decided to leave eBay and was determining what to do next. Everyone seemed to have their own thoughts about where I fit. The world was quick to say what was right for me, but none of it felt right. That changed when, years later, I met with Mitch Kapor and he introduced to me the possibility of working on my own and assembling my own team rather than joining someone else's. This insight shifted my whole worldview. My whole career, the world had been trying to manage me into conventional jobs, but I realized I didn't have to follow someone else's ideas for me. I could chart my own.

These are just some examples of what I call "the world trying to manage you into compliance." We are constantly being judged and categorized, but often this is based on "surfacey" things that may or may not matter. What really matters is what is the impact you are trying to make in the world and how committed are you to making it. As a founder, you likely find yourself in similar situations very frequently. When you encounter these situations, you should:

Consider the source. We are pummeled every day with junk mail, spam advertisements, and also, unsolicited advice. If you don't know or trust the source, you might want to disregard their input quickly.

Listen and ponder. If you do trust the source, you should listen and decide if they can sway your opinion of yourself and move you to do something differently. No one is perfect, and we need to be open to new input.

Decide whether you want to modify behavior as a result of the input. There are many times when I have definitely decided not to give in to what someone else wanted. But that's not always the right answer. Sometimes change is warranted.

If you decide not to accept the request, fully appreciate the comfort and satisfaction you feel in being yourself. Don't let others make you feel guilty about pursuing your goals.

Finally, while the world tries to manage you into compliance, it's up to you to pay attention to where you feel you need to go. You are the only person who understands what your true destiny is. Don't let anyone else's ideas and assumptions get in the way of that.

All the best,

Maynard

WHEN YOUR BOARD IS DRIVING YOU CRAZY

Dear Founder,

I'm sorry you're experiencing issues with your board. It's not fun. However, you have to fix it—because your directors won't. I've outlined ways to do so below, but first, let's take a step back to identify why this is happening.

Remember when you first created the board? This was at the beginning of the formation of the company, when everything was full of potential and it seemed that there was only upside. You decided to give up some control, probably in exchange for equity, and there was harmony. If a board member joined as the result of funding, there was likely peace and excitement at the moment, but these sentiments also came with certain expectations: namely, expectations around growth, market opportunity, leadership, and more.

Now, if there are problems, you need to understand how they occurred. One clue: It's likely that you haven't delivered on their expectations.

As with any relationship, the founder's relationship with the board changes over time.

While your board dynamic may start off amicably when your company is young, as your business grows, it's likely to encounter problems. How the CEO and the board deal with these problems determines everything.

In good times—you have a good quarter, you did what you said you would do—you and the board are in harmony. You can ask them to open doors, they cheer you on, and they challenge you to go faster. That's good board behavior.

Board dysfunction is usually preceded by company or CEO

dysfunction; it generally happens when the business or the CEO isn't doing well. It's not okay to dismiss this situation, thinking the board is being a pain and hoping they will go away. They will not go away, and it is their fiduciary duty to intervene and restore growth. Therefore, it's important to immediately identify the root cause of why the board is upset. A few things to consider:

Is this new behavior, or has it been going on for a while?

Is it that board meetings used to go well, but now you dread them? It's time to ask yourself: *What's changed?* Maybe it has to do with your last product shipment. Or perhaps you can't find a head of sales. Or it could be that customer reception is not what was expected. The result of any of these issues is that the board's trust in you has now shifted.

The board should know what's happening AND they should know what you are doing to fix it. Being defensive will not help. Problems do not have to be bad things—as long as you address them quickly. Put yourself in their shoes. What do you see?

- **Are there execution issues?** You said you'd hire a person and you didn't; you said you'd land customers that you didn't; you said the product would be released by a certain time, but it wasn't. If you have any of these execution issues, the board is banking on you to fix them.
- **Are there aspirational issues?** You said you'd become a market leader in nine months and you didn't. Aspirational issues are less fatal and can be resolved with the board over time.

Now, it's time to take a closer look at how you dealt with the issues, and how your response impacted your credibility. Questions to ask in a personal assessment include:

- Would my investors vote me onto the team if they were deciding today? Why or why not?
- If we were looking for funding would they re-up? Why or why not?
- Have I underperformed and made myself vulnerable to criticism and angst? Have I created a soft underbelly?
- What am I doing to show the board members that I've identified problems and am working to resolve them?

Also consider whether it's the whole board or just one member who is out of phase with everything else. If it's just one person:

- Do you know why they may be cranky? Sometimes, it's due to the other things going on that are not related to your company. How's their company or fund doing? What else is going on?
- Address the problem proactively. You may not have control over these issues, but you still have to deal with them. Call the board member to discuss the behavior privately. Share with them what you are experiencing and ask them what's going on to try to understand where they are coming from.
- You may also consider speaking with another trusted board member about this issue and asking them to reach out on your behalf.

You have to manage your board differently than you manage your customers and employees.

Your board has unique powers. Think about it. A customer can fire you, but you can get other customers. An employee can leave you, but you can find other employees. Board members? You are accountable to them, and they have the ability to fire you if things do not go well.

Too often, CEOs don't understand the board dynamics they walk into and therefore they have no idea to how to manage a board. A few things to keep in mind:

- Be realistic about what a board is and what it isn't, and how it functions.
- Be aware that you're gaining or losing credibility with a board every day. Just because you once had tons of trust and credibility, that doesn't mean that you can't lose it all very quickly. I once saw a public company CEO lose the support of his whole board in less than a week.
- Be able to predict where the board is on any given issue and why.

Navigating through board challenges is complicated and difficult. Here are five of the right moves to make:

1. **Be transparent with the board.** Some founders may be concerned that honesty makes them look weak. Not so. Tell the truth. Doing so will enable the board to trust you to accomplish your company's goals. Of course, I'm not suggesting that every time you have a bad night's sleep over a problem it requires board notification. You'll have to assess what is worth telling them. I'll give you some clues though: If there is a massive outage or something that will cause a loss in revenue, the board needs to know immediately. It's a little bit like managing any relationship. If I'm going to be home late, I'll be in trouble if I don't call. If I do call, I'll hear appreciation for the courtesy (most of the time). Don't forget to call when you are supposed to call.
2. **Put the board to work.** Your board is made up of the people who are closest to your company. They know your aspirations and your problems and they are aligned around

wanting you to succeed. Instead of doing all the work and just asking them to judge you, ask them to help you. Bring them into the loop so they can help problem-solve. Almost every board member wants to help.

- Tell them about the issue and the options you're considering. Ask what they would do if they were in your shoes.
- Ask them for their advice on your strategy and ask them to help open doors.

3. **Engage in dialogue, not debate.** Don't make it "us against them." Don't force them to a decision; encourage them to come along willingly. Make them feel as if they are part of the solution. This may mean taking two bites of the apple, not one. Instead of saying, "Here's what I've decided, and I need you to support it," try a two-step approach that offers them room to weigh in and provide their opinion. "I've been thinking about this . . ." and then, "What do you think about that idea?" This approach will bring them along on your journey.
4. **Know when to hold 'em and know when to fold 'em.** Not every decision should be given the same weight. You have to know when something is worth giving the sleeves off your vest. If this problem is a 10 on the Richter scale, you know best what you have to do. However, if it's a 2, let the board win. Trust gets burned on the small things that don't matter. Don't allow that to happen. Compromise on the small nits so you can retain trust and gain consensus on the big things (and read the next letter on picking your battles).
5. **Quickly determine whether or not the board is with you on the next steps.** Before every board meeting, check in with all the board members on the agenda topics and ask if there's anything else someone wants to cover. It's important

to understand all of the key issues in advance. We all know that sometimes someone comes in with a bee in their bonnet and they ruin the meeting! Avoid that. To do so, give them the chance to tell you where they're coming from and why.

- **Identify where everybody is.** Are they as excited today as when they invested in you? You should know.
- **Is their trust in you growing or shrinking, and why?** You need to know.
- **Do you have alignment around the cause of the problem and what is being done to solve it?**

Your relationship with your board is a long-term partnership, and in many ways is not too dissimilar from a marriage. To make it successful requires transparency, trust, more communication than imagined, and the willingness to compromise.

Also, remember that your partner is in a different position than you. Their job is to tell you what to do, and they don't have to deal with the consequences. Advising is easy, but execution is hard.

I've been in both roles and I can tell you, my perceived IQ went up ten points as soon as I became a board member because I didn't have to deal with the reality of anything I said. But for now, you do. Good luck and go get 'em!

All the best,

Maynard

WHEN YOU NEED TO PICK YOUR BATTLES

Dear Founder,

If you're like most founders, you likely have very clear opinions on what your company's vision, product, strategy, and culture, should look like. And every day will bring new potential sources of conflict on any number of fronts. If you have the answers already, shouldn't you just bend disagreements to your way of thinking?

Difficult as it may be in practice, fighting every battle is not a smart strategy. The old adage that you can win every battle and still lose the war is true. Throughout my career, I've learned that you can't fight and argue about everything you disagree with, as this will leave you exhausted and, worse, it will eat away at the trust others place in you. Remember, you are building or losing credibility every day. You must really know which decisions are worth imposing your will on—and which ones aren't. This is something I employ every day at my boards, where there are many issues that arise, but only a small number of decisions I force. I choose to let many things go so that I can have a say in the big issues that I believe will determine the future of the company.

This doesn't mean that you shouldn't ever fight for what you want. It does mean you need to determine what things are worth fighting for. Recently, a WIN portfolio company CEO was trying to remove one of his board members, and was fighting with his third board member about what to do. The issue? They were right in the midst of trying to sell the company! What trumps what?

If I were the CEO in this situation, I would put up with some dysfunction on the board and focus instead on the prize of selling the company. Fighting to remove someone I didn't like would likely screw up the outcome I actually wanted. (Not to mention, trying to remove a board member can backfire, and might lead to my ouster instead! Much worse.) Choosing the wrong battle will burn cycles and pull you away from achieving your true goals.

How do you know what's worth it and what's not? I look to the great Stephen Covey's work delineating the difference between a "sphere of influence" and "circle of concern." We are all upset by the crises we hear about every day: outdated infrastructure, new epidemics, housing shortages. These are horrible. Yet for most people who aren't elected officials or can't vote in these cities, these issues fall within a circle of concern: We can give money and volunteer our time, but these are likely not situations where we can have significant influence.

If you want to effect change, it's better to focus on the areas where you have a sphere of influence. So, if you're concerned about inequaity in this country, instead of going after things at a national level, make the changes in your company—where you have the influence and power to make a difference.

Another necessary thing to note is the importance of training your team to make great decisions and understand their consequences. This kind of education will lead to fewer contentious battles. For example, when I was at eBay, we went to Telluride, Colorado, to participate in strategy and budget planning each year. After Meg Whitman and I shared our strategic options with all our top execs, we then asked them to act as if they were board members, and vote on which initiatives to pursue. It was empowering for them and helped them grow perspective. While only the exec staff and board actually voted and approved the strategy and plan, we found the broader input from execs to be not only rewarding for them, but also very informative for us. And having their buy-in went a long way when it came to executing these strategies.

How do you tell if something is in your circle of concern or sphere of influence? Ask yourself the following questions:

1. Is it in my scope? Is this my responsibility? Is this something I have to do? Is it an opportunity to let someone else lead and learn?
2. How important is this decision? Is it a company decision where there are great stakes? Or, is this an experiment? If it doesn't work out, will it be uncomfortable, or will it be a catastrophe?

You always have to weigh in if something is a make-or-break decision for the company. If it isn't, understand that you have a million things to decide, and one of the best decisions you can make is deciding when to jump in and when to let go.

All the best,

Maynard

WHEN YOU WANT TO BLAME SOMEONE

Dear Founder,

I know how it feels when you're angry that something didn't go right. You may even feel justified in pointing fingers at the person or people you believe let you down. Or, you may even think it would be appropriate to publicly shame them for disappointing you and the company.

I understand that what they did was bad—maybe very bad—and now it's causing you all sorts of problems. Instinctually you want to blame someone. However, you can't be so quick to blame them or act on that feeling of blame. Maybe this sounds like a small thing, but this is a real issue that can derail executives and leaders.

This was a lesson I learned early on. I remember playing American Legion Baseball when I was eighteen years old. We were a very good team and made it to the state championships. I adored our coach who was very funny and inspirational most of the time. Yet, I will never forget his speech when we were eliminated after losing our first two games in the state finals: "I guess you can't make chicken salad out of chicken shit." His rant was clearly not a very inspirational way to end what was a good season that could have been great. It taught me that losing sucks, but there is still a way to be gracious about it and get inspired by the experience. Instead of inspiration and hope for the future, our coach delivered bitterness and blame.

Now, as a senior executive and board member, I've seen a number of executives throw other people under the bus. This action almost always ends up looking bad for the executive who does it—not the team member who made the mistake. The executive should be a good enough manager to know the importance of reflecting on the problem, owning up to their piece of the accountability, and focusing on the learning. I keep an eye out for executives who are quick to blame others, and I try to coach them on correcting this flaw.

You will never build credibility with your whole team when you don't go into these situations with a "beginner's mind." Instead of quickly jumping into the blame game, look at everything as if it's the first time you saw it. Ask yourself:

- What happened here?
- What did we miss?
- How could I have helped to see this earlier and help fix it faster?
- How likely is this to happen again?

Build a culture of openness and learning for your teams. Have employees be tougher on themselves than anyone else. Such behavior typically happens when you create a transparent AND supportive culture where mistakes are generally used as learning experiences and everyone is encouraged to be brutally honest about how they are doing.

When something doesn't go well, dive deep into why and focus on the learnings—instead of the blaming. For example, during a postmortem from a system outage, are you looking for gaps in process and execution to shore them up in order to avoid a recurrence, or are you quick to fire someone who made a mistake? (Of course, as I've said before, if you have employees or leaders who aren't learners or high achievers, you must let them go. Allow them to be mediocre somewhere else. Or, perhaps they will become stars in a different environment.)

Your environment should enable learning, practice forgiveness, and foster inspiration. There's an old, but true, adage: When you point a finger, three point back at you. It is so much better to take more ownership of an issue even if you sometimes don't feel it is warranted. I remember we had a big outage at eBay a few years into my tenure. In the past, Meg Whitman had terminated other executives, in the middle of a crisis, for similar problems. However, this time she was working with a new team and we had made a lot of progress and had earned her trust. We knew we had to deliver and she knew she had to as well. She worked very closely with us through the outage and she told us how proud she was of the progress we had made. Instead of feeling that she blamed us and instead of worrying about losing our jobs, we were inspired to fix the problem and to not let Meg or our customers down.

No one does their best work when they feel that they are on the edge. No one will take chances or strive to be better when they live in fear. So, instead of seeking revenge by throwing someone under the bus, transform that urge into preventing the situation the next time around and inspire everyone to do better.

All the best,

Maynard

WHEN YOU ARE ASKED TO KEEP SOMETHING IN CONFIDENCE

Dear Founder,

When someone asks you to keep something in confidence, you want to say yes—but this is never a black-and-white issue. More often than not, it's a million shades of gray.

Maybe they want to tell you that you are at risk of losing a key employee. (You should not throw the person telling you this information under the bus, but you should find a way to check in with the employee.) Perhaps someone wants to tell you that they are going through a divorce. (Express your sympathy; ask what you can do to help them, such as offering more flexibility so that they can pick up their kids.) What if they want to confess that they did something illegal, unethical, or immoral? (Thank them for their candor, but also clarify that you still have to take action.)

I've experienced some gnarly and less-than-straightforward issues myself. Recently, someone I admire greatly asked me to be a reference, and I had to keep this a big secret. That sounds simple, but it was incredibly complex since they are currently in a big job. In another example, a line executive came to me in my capacity as a board member with a complaint about the CEO. He had not talked to the CEO yet, and I sent him back to do so.

Situations like this happen. While each one is unique and requires judgment, there are some ground rules to consider that may help you navigate these choppy waters:

- **First, understand that the only way to be given trust is to deserve it.** While you will often be "in the know" on interesting things, you should, in general, totally honor the request for confidentiality. That is what I did with the above job reference. During my time at Yahoo! there were all kinds of leaks, often from outside the company. Reporters often called me to check these rumors and offered that my comments could be "off the record." I never did that. My responsibility was to Yahoo! and its shareholders, and I never wanted to violate the board policy on communication outside of the company.

- **Be clear that it's not as simple as a pinky swear.** I always make clear to people who are going to tell me something that I generally have a fiduciary obligation, which may require me to take an action. For example, if someone tells me about a bribe, sexual harassment, or some other illegal activity, I am obligated to take action. I will do my best to respect their wishes for privacy, but I will have to do what I'm legally and morally bound to do.

Be upfront about how you will handle confidences and then live up to them. It takes a long time to build trust, but it can be broken in an instant. Keep both your integrity and your fiduciary obligations front and center. Doing so will serve you well.

All the best,

Maynard

WHEN YOU NEED TO BURN THE CLOCK

Dear Founder,

In many sports that depend on a clock—think football and basketball—when a team gets ahead and it's close to the end of the game, they often do everything they can to stall and keep the ball away from the other party. This practice is called burning the clock. The reverse situation exists when the clock is running down and you're behind. Here is when your hurry-up offense comes in!

In business, a similar set of circumstances happens relatively frequently. You may find yourself wanting to burn the clock:

- **When you're doing a deal or any kind of negotiation.** The best chances for a great outcome usually require having multiple parties bidding or negotiating. There is often one bidder that becomes the favorite, but it's incumbent on the buyer to keep multiple bidders happy and engaged. We had nine serious bidders in the Yahoo! sale process. All were watching for signals or signs that indicated if they were preferred or if they were not being seriously considered. We ended up with five finalists and worked hard to ensure all of them felt that they were on a level playing field.
- **When you're hiring.** You may have a preferred candidate, but you must keep the pipeline of other candidates warm in case something doesn't work out.
- **When someone has quit.** Often this person becomes a "persona non grata" in the company. I would rather have that individual fully engaged and working hard all the way through the rest of their tenure. If that means I need to keep being professional and polite—and put aside the fact that I may be disappointed—that's a small price to pay. When I quit Figgie International, the head of HR was very upset

> with me. He made it clear that I shouldn't play in the daily basketball game over lunch that I usually participated in. I became somewhat of a pariah and it was pretty uncomfortable. Yet it turned out to be a temporary banishment. He came to see me a few days after he made his point and welcomed me back to play. It was nice, even if I was fouled a little more often than usual!

When you commit to burning the clock, you are consciously agreeing to spend time on something (e.g., third preferred bidder or second-choice candidate) that is not likely to bear fruit—but this work is required to achieve your ultimate best outcome. I have found that rather than being annoyed about spending time this way, I feel far better about it when I remind myself that this effort is contributing to my ultimate goal.

Here's to becoming a master at burning the clock!

All the best,

Maynard

6

External Roadblocks

WHEN A COMPETITOR ENTERS YOUR SPACE

GUEST LETTER BY ADAM GOLDSTEIN, CO-FOUNDER AND CEO, HIPMUNK, A WEBB INVESTMENT NETWORK PORTFOLIO COMPANY

Dear Founder,

When you started your company, you were familiar with the existing competition, and you had an idea of how you might beat them. Yet sometimes, out of nowhere, an established company in a different industry decides to start competing in yours. It can come as a particularly nasty surprise and the news causes chatter both inside and outside your company, and it's not clear how—or even whether—you should respond.

Less than six months after we launched Hipmunk flight search, Google spent $700 million to acquire a different travel company and start building a product that competed directly with ours. The announcement came with little warning and raised doubts among our investors, employees, and even my co-founder and me.

You might be tempted to give up on your company in hopelessness, but be careful not to overreact. An announcement isn't the same as an existential threat, and when a big company rushes to market in a space it doesn't know well, the product is rarely compelling right away.

Assuming you decide to plow ahead with your company, here are some things to keep in mind:

Accept that fundraising will get harder for a while.

Here's a tip: When every investor asks you if you're worried about a new competitor, you can be sure that all of *them* are worried about the new competitor.

More to the point, every investor is worried that every other investor is worried. That matters a lot. When investor sentiment turns on an industry, even promising companies struggle to raise money because investors don't want to fund a company that won't be able to find future investors. In this way, investor worries can become self-fulfilling.

There's no way around it: This is bad news for you. Don't pretend nothing has changed; recognize you need to change your approach.

If you don't need to raise money, consider waiting. Everyone assumes the worst when news first hits, but when the world sees the shortfalls in your competitor's effort, you may find investor sentiment turn in your favor again. If you do need to raise money, consider looking for less and lowering your valuation expectations.

Consider also talking to established companies in your industry, which might themselves feel threatened by the new entrant. They might be willing to invest in you as a hedge.

Also, read the "When you have a crisis" letter!

The enemy of your enemy may be your friend.

The funny thing about Google entering the travel industry was that it scared everyone else in the industry into working together in ways they never would have considered before.

Besides investing in startups as a hedge (see above), established companies like Priceline and Expedia did partnership deals left and right with companies that they thought could give them an edge against Google. For those startups with the right combination of skill and luck, the entrance of Google was a blessing in disguise.

Look for the companies in your industry that have the most to lose from the new entrant. Start regular conversations with them. You never know what might happen.

Set the right tone with your investors and employees.

When big companies enter a new space, they sometimes fail, but they usually don't fail right away. For better or worse, you should expect to see this company continuing to make headlines in your industry for a while.

That's why it's important to set a tone of respect and curiosity right from the start. Not dismissal and derision, but also not obsession and despair.

Don't wait for investors and employees to ask what it all means. Talk to them proactively. Tell them, truthfully, that you view it as a sign that the market you're in is a big opportunity. Acknowledge that it may mean new challenges, but demonstrate the optimism that you can overcome them, just as you've overcome past challenges. Make sure everyone feels that you're in touch with what's going on, and also feels reassured that you're not overly perturbed.

Over time, you may be able to learn things from your competitor's approach. Use their products, and talk to customers about what they like about them. Encourage your employees to do the same. Keep in mind there's so much you don't know yet about your competitor's strategy. For the sake of your credibility, don't pretend you have it all figured out.

Finally, depending on how threatening the new company is, you may even be able to use them as a rallying cry for your team. You, the David to their Goliath, are slowly beating them.

Be ready for more.

When one big company moves, other big companies often follow. Brace yourself for more surprises like this one.

In anticipation, consider reaching out to other companies *before* they enter your space. You may find them interested in partnering or investing.

But also keep in mind that tech industries don't remain ultracompetitive forever. Sooner or later, companies will die, or else merge to build up scale. The same fundraising headwinds you're facing are going to affect everyone else, too. Keep an eye out for good companies that you can buy up cheap.

Finally, as odd as it might sound, make friends with your new competitor. They're entering your industry because they're interested in your industry. Maybe their first product will be a failure, but they'll still be interested in the industry as a whole, and you'll be growing by leaps and bounds. Maybe their first product will be a success but you serve a slightly different market segment and they'll realize they want the expertise you have.

You're in a battle, even more so than before the recent news. Make the most of your chances by moving fast and making allies.

All the best,

Adam Goldstein
Co-founder, CEO Hipmunk

WHEN YOU NEED TO BE MANIACALLY FOCUSED ON YOUR BUSINESS

Dear Founder,

So, you're worried about competition?

If you are just starting out, don't be! If you worry too much about what you are up against, you will never start something new. We'd still buy tickets through travel agents instead of online, we'd still use taxis instead of Uber or Lyft, and there would be no Facebook—only a failed Myspace. Competition—whether you're competing against another company or the status quo—is what evolves old ideas, inspires new ones, and makes the world work better.

If you are scaling and building a legacy company, you should be aware of and prepared for competition—it's relentless and companies do crazy things to gain market share from one another—but this isn't something most startup founders have to be hyperfocused on. The problem with putting too much emphasis on the competition is that it causes us to lose sight of where we are going. It's hard to run up the stairs when one is always looking right and left, and constantly checking to see who might be coming up from behind. What is important is to stay grounded in your vision or strategy—not that you try to keep up with someone else's. Remember, you are the one in control of the narrative about who you are and where you are going.

The week I officially joined eBay, and it was still a new (and struggling) company, Microsoft and Dell launched an online auction site called FairMarket. Everyone was very worried about this initiative. We wondered: *Could this be the end of eBay?*

Obviously, we now know how this story ends: Just because you have a big name doesn't mean you will get a big win. FairMarket never became a real threat and eBay wound up buying it a few years later. Had we gotten bogged down in competing against them, we would have lost track of what we were doing, changed our strategy to account for their influence, and given them validation in the market they didn't warrant. It was more powerful to focus on what we wanted.

We had built a true global marketplace where consumers found items they wanted and entrepreneurs (sellers) found new markets for their products. FairMarket was intended to be a place where large companies could move their products. We were the place at that time where people came to shop. And, we decided to stay focused on this approach and how to become better at it. We prioritized what was most important: scalability (we had significant service issues due to our growth), trust (we had to make transactions safer for consumers), friction (most of the payments were by check or money order as opposed to PayPal), and user experience. We also expanded into multiple countries, either via new launches (like in the United Kingdom) or acquisition (like in Germany). So, while we kept an eye on what the competition was doing, we spent most of our time making our successful service better, safer, easier to use, and more global.

That experience showed the value in knowing what is going on around you, but not letting it disable you. Be acutely aware of markets and customers, and listen to what they are telling you. And more importantly, you need to be able to predict where they are heading.

But you must be more focused on what you want to achieve and constantly working to get better. (The path to achievement rests on setting aggressive yet achievable goals and monitoring results.) You are your most important competition. If *you* don't build a product or service of relevance, it really doesn't matter what your competition does. I always find inspiration in sports: As Michael Jordan said, "You have competition every day because you set such high standards for yourself that you have to go out every day and live up to that." That attitude is how he got to be one of the greatest basketball players of all time—and it's really the secret for anyone to succeed.

All the best,

Maynard

WHEN YOU RECEIVE PUBLIC CRITICISM

Dear Founder,

"There's no such thing as bad press" is an oft-cited and much-debated mantra. There are some who believe any publicity is good publicity, while others rally against the phrase, claiming it is untrue and an unwelcome license to engage in outlandish behavior. (See anything on E!, the entertainment network.)

While I strive to keep my head low and receive only positive recognition, I've come to realize that getting input—good or bad—is a blessing. It gives you invaluable information on how you are doing, and more importantly, how you can do better. Even bad press, while it can be uncomfortable, can also be an incredible opportunity for improvement.

So what do you do when you're on the receiving end of critical reviews or negative comments? First of all, congrats—this is validation that people care about what you're doing. It's confirmation that you have some traction. People who aren't engaged won't talk about you or your product or service.

But there's no time to enjoy this realization; you must immediately aim to make the situation right.

First, you must assess the impact. Is this a story that will just blow over or is this one that must be addressed? Early in my tenure at Yahoo! we faced an issue over our CEO. Some thought it would blow over quickly, which, of course, it didn't. If it is a big issue, address it. If it's one that should be ignored, ignore it. When United Airlines personnel dragged a passenger off a plane, the world was outraged. The CEOs initial response, which defended the airline's actions, fueled the flames.

If customers are discussing the issue in print, on the web, on social media, on external sites, or on your site, you must understand that they believe that their opinions are important, and you should listen.

When you get this heat, you have to lean into the fire and respond immediately. That's the best way to put it out. Be open and transparent about the issue; do not try to bury it, and do not think it will go away. Problems, like a stinky cheese, get more potent with age. Responding in a timely manner is a better approach. Specifically:

1. Don't get defensive. It doesn't look good and doesn't help correct matters.
2. Acknowledge the issue at hand, appropriately apologize for any missteps, and let people know what you are doing to correct it.
3. Ensure your critics feel as though you've heard their point of view. You may not agree, and that's okay. Only after they've felt heard, should you make your point of view known.

I saw the value of putting this plan in place during a tough situation at eBay when we had a twenty-two-hour outage. Meg Whitman had the whole company call customers and apologize. She also promised them a free listing day as soon as the site could handle the load. Salesforce looked to eBay's playbook when it struggled with service interruptions. The company created a trust site where anyone could see the status of the service. That transparent approach built trust with customers. (Of course, the complaints only went down when things actually got better!)

No company will escape criticism, but how they deal with it is what makes all the difference. A few years ago, when Zendesk's customers complained about a change in pricing, the company grandfathered existing customers into the old pricing, then offered a public apology. That meant something to the customers. As one commenter responded to the Zendesk letter: "You know, this type of thing is why we picked Zendesk in the first place . . . a company who listens to its users. It's curious, after this episode, I'm even more happy with the company."

When your biggest critics are customers, remember: *Most of the time, they don't actually want to be spending their time criticizing you.* An angry user is a user who loved your business, and feels betrayed somehow. Salve their concerns, and you'll reaffirm their loyalty. Make them feel included when you do have problems and challenges, and they not only will cut you slack, they might even help you solve the problem.

While not an example from the tech world, there's a famous story from Domino's Pizza I always liked. A few years ago, Domino's Pizza had a great reputation for pricing and speed, but a terrible one for quality. Rather than ignore customer feedback, the company decided in 2010 to address the pizza's poor quality. In one web spot, CEO Patrick Doyle said, "There comes a time when you know you gotta make a change." An executive read comment cards with consumers' critiques, including, "Worst excuse for pizza I've ever had." Doyle promised to learn and to "get better." The company built pizzaturnaround.com, where visitors could post their thoughts publicly and Domino's could learn and respond. In what's perhaps the move that made the pizza chain the most vulnerable, it took over a giant digital billboard in New York's Times Square and invited any customer who ordered pizza via the internet through the company's Domino's Pizza Tracker app to have their feedback broadcasted on the big screen for everyone to see. All comments were welcome, even the harsh ones. The result of their reaction to criticism: better pizza and better business. The company saw an immediate increase in domestic sales and a jump in its stock price.

While negative press can present difficult challenges—and sometimes have serious negative long-term ramifications—companies that face these challenges head-on emerge better off. They discover that they have passionate customers who care deeply about their business and products, and by listening and responding, these companies earn their customers' loyalty and continue to grow.

Want to create evangelists? Consistently deliver an amazing product that people love. And if you do something wrong, make it right. Negative sentiment is not a reason to retreat under the covers, but rather an amazing opportunity to show customers what you really are offering: a commitment to do everything you can to delight them.

All the best,

Maynard

WHEN YOU NEED TO MANAGE THE LAWSUIT FILED AGAINST YOUR COMPANY

GUEST LETTER BY MONTGOMERY KERSTEN, JD, STANFORD LAW SCHOOL, 1980, FORMER FORTUNE 500 GENERAL COUNSEL, INVOLVED IN FAMOUS LITIGATION

Dear Founder,

How should you manage the lawsuit just filed against your company? Do not be alarmed: a lawsuit is not lethal; it's just a thorn in a paw that needs to be removed.

Now, take a deep breath, push away your anger and indignation, and keep calm and carry on (as the British are fond of saying). Being served with a lawsuit is a "red badge of courage" that many ventures experience—in a bizarre way, it declares: "You have arrived."

Most important: View this threat as just another business problem to be managed by the CEO. It is primarily a business problem, secondarily a "legal" problem. Don't let any of your constituents worry about it; rather, get it out of their minds ASAP (there's no upside in being a lawsuit defendant).

Having recognized that, as the CEO, your first question in considering how to manage this lawsuit should be: What are the business goals I wish to achieve for the company in managing this lawsuit? Emotion has no role in answering this question. And note: Lawsuits, by their nature, detract from and harm your focus on achieving your business goals in your operating plan. They are dangerous and parasitic and nonproductive. They require your acute attention.

How you proceed is all about managing the case; it is not about "attacking" or "prove them wrong" or "millions for defense, not a penny for tribute!"

Be clear in your mind about what your business goals are in resolving the lawsuit. Be dispassionate and seek to "get rid" of it, and not make it a "showdown at the O.K. Corral." Young ventures with only a few millions in cash in the bank simply can't afford multi-year lawsuits, and thus their strategies in dealing with them are wholly different from the big boys like the Fortune 500 that have already allocated multiple millions a year in the "business as usual" litigation budgets from their big legal departments. Most Fortune 500's view their litigation budget as a "blunt-edged weapon," which they invoke without paying attention to the merits of the cases they bring or defend. They are instead designed to destroy competition, with the advantage of a war chest (you have no war chest for lawyers).

Understand that the world of courts and judges and lawyers is a twilight zone; it is not a "business" zone, and thus, the normal, rational rules of business do not apply.

Don't believe the portrayal of the law as depicted on TV programs—that's utter fantasy. Instead, as a CEO responsible for preserving cash and building shareholder value, you cannot employ mere logic or business judgment to direct your actions. No, this is the unique legal forum, which has perpetuated from time immemorial (Martial, the court poet of the Emperor Nero complained two thousand years ago of "the law's bitter tedious cases," and Shakespeare lamented the "law's delay" in Hamlet's famous soliloquy). Thus, do not turn to "common sense" as a rule of how to proceed: rather, you must hire the very best, experienced, and clever lawyer possible (not necessarily the best name or law firm in the business or the most expensive) to lead this business problem to resolution (more on that below).

Yet, before retaining the "right" lawyer (it is not a law firm you hire, as much as retaining a specific partner you trust, who will care about your business more than his bills—a veteran partner you believe in), it is critical to be aware that any time a venture suffers a lawsuit, it has two problems to contend with:

1. The "enemy" lawyers who will do all they can to twist the facts and the law and the merits, while dragging your cycles and billing your opponent to the max to win against you, despite truth being against them.
2. Your own lawyers who by the nature of their business model, don't want a quick fix, and instead often wish to extract as much money from your venture representing you in this case as they can accomplish while they hold your hand and say, "We are doing all we can!" (that is what "litigators" do) all the while getting you to think they are your savior, perhaps leading you to longer-term ruin convincing you they will prevail, rather than just settling.

Thus, it is critical that you retain a lawyer in a firm that you trust will place your business goals above their revenue/billing goals, and that both the lawyer and the firm value a long-term relationship with your venture far past the resolution of this case.

As important: Both must know the court you are in, must know the opponent law firm, and must know the judge well (we prefer if they play golf together).

Know what you are dealing with: the court system in America.

I often tell founders: Going to trial is dangerous no matter the merits and no matter the facts you think are in your favor. I'd rather be in a Las Vegas casino betting my venture's money and future on the craps table where I understand the odds, than in a courtroom in front of a judge and jury, and a clever enemy lawyer, even if I am sure I'm right and "should" win. Do not believe that courts are the engine of truth—they are subject to human frailty and uncertainty and its consequent flaws and tears of "how could that have happened?"

Thus, startups almost never go to trial because it just costs too darn much (a lawsuit going to trial can cost as much as $2–4 million a year for a young venture), and the risks are often too great, and your case could backfire! And they suck unproductive cycles from all your team, and even your customers (not to mention your cash balance). Lawsuits are chess games, not checkers. They move slowly, and you must anticipate the next ten moves, and countermoves of your opponent. I tell founders that litigation is the sport of kings; sure, Apple and Samsung can afford multiyear patent battles (Apple's law firm bill was over $60 million as publicly reported), but startups cannot afford to pay even a million dollars for any lawsuit defense. So, a lawsuit for a young venture (that you are defending, not bringing) is something to dispose of without losing, as rapidly as possible. Kind of like dog doo-doo on your shoe—get rid of it.

Thus, you should immediately assess:

- What are the business goals of the enemy plaintiff company (and its lawyers) in bringing this lawsuit?
- What are your business goals in resisting and disposing of the lawsuit?
- What is the best way to reach a resolution (whether settlement or go to trial)?

In devising an initial strategy for responding and managing, keep these guides in mind:

1. Immediately defuse this public lawsuit in the eyes of your employees, investors, and customers (if needed to reach that far); be proactive in managing the PR of the lawsuit;

don't let it become a PR problem, nor an employee or a customer-relations problem, in addition to being a legal threat. Your goal should be to get it off their collective radar screen as rapidly as possible. A lawsuit is public knowledge, by its nature, so get proactive on how to respond, but keep in mind, the goal should be to take it out of the public mind as time progresses—don't get into a PR pissing match.

2. Rapidly retain counsel you trust (see above) and tell them everything under attorney/client privilege—your lawyer must know all the facts and the secrets and the issues behind it, and most of all constantly remind your lawyer of your business goals in resolving the suit.
3. Quickly construct with your law firm the next ninety days of actions—assess the hope of marshaling a counterclaim against the plaintiff where, carefully and deliberately you may be able to determine a claim by your venture against the enemy, to put them back on their heels and begin to rethink "Was it a good idea to sue these guys?" You don't want to be just on the defensive, but you should not bring meritless counterclaims, which will merely undermine your credibility and fuel the flames of a fire you wish to extinguish.
4. Push your law firm to consider aggressive, judo-like strategies and tactics that force a resolution. Seek a win-win possible settlement where your opponent and you can both look like you "won." And consider SOON getting aggressive about "discovery" where you seek to depose under penalty of perjury the senior executives of your opponent (after you have developed enough facts through interrogatories and other early discovery tactics). When the senior execs of your enemy find themselves under the microscope of your lawyers in a deposition room, their ap-

petite for litigation often suddenly is lost. Many law firms save this move for a year or two into the litigation, but I like to notice the depositions of the top execs of my opponent ASAP.

5. Stay on top of this as the CEO. Do not just delegate it to your CFO—lawsuits are dangerous, unpredictable, and can become boomerangs for all involved. Make sure you personally have a solid relationship with your law firm and the lead partner, where you drive them to focus on your business goals for the litigation and your cost-containment goals.

Cost control is critical. Mandate that the law firm you retain cannot staff this case with more than three lawyers: the lead partner, a junior partner, and one associate (and a paralegal).

I have prevailed with that staff against enemy firms with truly ten times those numbers—we were so more on top of the case than those many minions! And, know each of your lean staff's billing rates. Review their monthly bills and question them (it makes a difference or they will bill as much as they can). Also, make sure you provide in the revised operating plan of your company for your best estimate of the ongoing expense, so your board is aware and you plan for it without destroying your cash plan.

Litigation is WAR.

Treat it that way: Go for the jugular of your opponent. Seek to kill them or neutralize them, rapidly. Yet, given that you are a small company, think: JUDO! Many a case can be resolved early on if you think out of the box, with a mind to what the enemy seeks, and what it fears. I've resolved cases for almost nothing, where dignity and honor and "mutual peace" prevailed, in light of the plaintiff's goals (plus a magnum of champagne for the opponent). And if no compromise is possible, then do all you can to destroy the enemy while NOT distracting your company from achieving its business model. If your enemy is determined to destroy you no matter what, then delay and counterattack are the best tactics.

Do not give management of the case to your law firm; rather, manage their response to the lawsuit just as if it is a plan to build and launch a new product: with a plan, and a schedule, and a budget, and milestone reviews, while always being guided by the unemotional business mandate.

Sincerely,

Montgomery Kersten

WHEN YOUR IDEA JUST ISN'T WORKING

Dear Founder,

Well, if you've opened this letter, things are not going well.

I'm sorry that things are off-kilter; it's never easy. We back brilliant founders all the time, and unfortunately, through a combination of flawed execution, poor market timing, or unanticipated exogenous factors, many seed-stage companies just never get off the ground.

At this point, the most important thing is to figure out what you are going to do about it.

I recently met with an entrepreneur who's been working on—and investing his own money in—an idea he's passionate about. He's been at it for more than twelve months and the business is not yet fundable by outside investors. The problem? It's a consumer product in a noisy space and it still doesn't have much traction. This worries me profoundly and it's clear that he needs to make a change. I reminded him of the obvious: His time and his savings are very important assets. I asked him to think about how he was investing these resources and to come up with the concrete steps that would lead him to success in a short period of time.

If you are in a similar situation, the following are some of realities for you to ponder as you decide how to proceed:

- **You never get the time you are spending back.** Are you spending your precious time on something that will produce world impact or deliver multigenerational wealth? If not, you may want to tweak things so that you are.
- **Are you spending every dollar wisely and with impact?** Being thoughtful about how you spend is another incredible resource and you need to know that you are handling it well.

- **How is your team holding up?** Are they fired up, and ready to go out swinging? Silicon Valley is filled with temptation for talented employees, so it's crucial to know how committed your people are.

Given those truths: *Should you keep on trucking?* All entrepreneurs hit hard times and tough choices, but many have survived precisely because they stayed with the same idea. Ben Silbermann made incremental changes to improve Pinterest, but he kept the vision and didn't pivot from the idea of a social bulletin board. Marc Benioff evolved Salesforce by bringing popular consumer trends to the enterprise, but never pivoted away from his idea of making software easier, more accessible, and more democratic for businesses. Before you completely change course, there could be other correctional steps to take such as tweaking a product, increasing marketing activities, or ramping up sales spend. Salesforce certainly made all of these modifications.

Should you think about a pivot?

Some great entrepreneurs have executed a "big pivot," changing everything about the product. Instagram, which started as Burbn, a mobile social check-in app with game features, saw that the photo-sharing feature was where the majority of its user engagement came from and pivoted to deliver on that before launch. When we invested in Meteor, it was only a few weeks after they had pivoted from building a travel guide for iPad. They realized that they were again re-creating front-end syncing technology that they had already built twice before and they decided to focus on that instead. When we backed GOAT, it was after Grubwithus founders, Eddy Lu and Daishin Sugano, had spent three years leanly trying to make social dining work, stepped back, reevaluated, and decided to use their team to create a marketplace dedicated to selling high-end sneakers.

Despite the success stories, pivots are not always the obvious next step or a guaranteed route to success. I would only suggest pivoting if you have a great team and a great idea to chase. Remember, you are now deciding to use investor money and the team's time on something that was not the original premise for the company.

Is it time to shut it down?

Sometimes there are no more steps you can take and the most responsible solution is to call it quits because you're burning time and cash (your investors' and your own), and there's little hope left that you can make something magical happen. In this case, you will want to return as much cash as possible and find your next thing.

What's your next move? It's time to take a hard look at everything. The answers to the following questions should give you some clarity and be able to guide you to the right next move. In this situation, you should ask yourself:

- **How long do you have to live?** How much cash do you have to continue pursuing your dream? Can you raise more money based on the traction you have?
- **Is there traction at all?** Are you building something that people like? How certain are you that this will be a winnable market? Are you early? Late? Is your timing off?
- **Can you do something that has much more relevance?** Have you developed any new insights that demonstrate that you should be chasing something else, ideally something you and your team have seen is a clear need? If you can: *Is your team the right one to execute on this idea?*
- **How do you want to treat those who have invested in you when you are unsure of where you want to go?** Are you able to provide a return to shareholders rather than just burn through the cash?

- **Most importantly:** ***What are you prepared to take on?*** A pivot means starting all over again—fundraising, recruiting, hyping what you've built. If that prospect doesn't fire you up, it may be time to look elsewhere.

I'm sorry that you are in this situation and at a crossroads. Dig deep, and decide whether you need to make some tweaks (modifications), execute a pivot, or to shut things down. Amazon founder and CEO Jeff Bezos calls this "investigate everything" process the "regret-minimization framework," and he encourages his teams to explore all the plausible possibilities—spending extra time to determine if the idea is worth it, rather than having regrets about giving up too early or not diving deep enough.

And don't forget, there are plenty of people who have been through this before. Ask trusted investors, other founders, and family or friends to put their "friend" hats on. What would they do in your shoes? Reflect, make up your mind, and get going.

All the best,

Maynard

PART III

GETTING TO SCALE

7
Operational Excellence

WHEN YOU NEED TO IMPROVE EXECUTION

Dear Founder,

I'm sure that you're finding it hard to accept that people are not delivering on their commitments. Personally, I find this behavior to be the one that causes me the most angst. People are either gaining credibility or losing credibility every day. The absolute best way to increase your credibility is to deliver what you say you are going to do.

One of my mentors and my manager at IBM, John Frandsen, used to say, "You can't expect what you don't inspect." I took this advice to heart and spent a lot of time ensuring that I knew where everything was and made sure that we surfaced any issues early and fixed them fast. I was relentless at checking in and became known for demanding high expectations that resulted in delivering quality on tough deadlines. It was good for people's career growth, but it wasn't for the faint of heart. I was so driven and on top of things that often I was also accused of being a micromanager.

As my career evolved and the organizations that I was involved with grew, I realized that I needed to implement practices and a culture that ensured execution happened without my direct involvement on every piece. I needed to ensure things got done without micromanaging.

Over time, I learned how to do that and I saw the results. I took pride when my teams delivered things that others found impossible. When I was at eBay, I saw a tech team achieve greatness against the odds. At one point, we had issues with getting search to scale to keep up with the incredible rate at which we were adding new listings to the site. Typically, it took twenty-four hours to index description listings before they went live, angering sellers who were paying for the service. In addition, the infrastructure updates cost the company millions. Solving this technology puzzle was not eBay's core competency, so the management team looked to buy a solution rather than build it. We approached Google and Yahoo! but ultimately, given the uniqueness of our needs and the urgency of the situation, we decided to build it ourselves. The developer team knew its mission and didn't have to be driven hard. They were self-motivated, inspired, and engaged to create change. What should have been a twelve- to eighteen-month project was achieved in six months. The newly built solution allowed us to get listings up in minutes and saved us millions of dollars.

I've also experienced firsthand how much can get done when you are not in normal times—when you're in crisis. And I've come to realize how in normal circumstances we set goals that are just average and uninspiring. It was far from normal circumstances in the aftermath of 9/11. That afternoon, then-Governor Pataki called and asked if we could auction items that were given to the state of New York and then send the proceeds to charities. What about doing something more compelling, we asked? What about firing up our community of sellers to help set up an auction and raise money for victims of the disaster? We had never done a project of this kind, which we soon named Auction for America. We needed to get toll-free 800 numbers and create the capability for people to answer the calls. (Previously we had relied on emails.) There were also tax considerations and government regulatory issues and approvals we needed. And on top of that, the coding itself was massively complex. In the past, this project would have taken us six months, but we didn't have that kind of time. And it turned out—as the team showed us—we didn't need it. We worked night and day, literally, for four nights. Maybe that sounds hellacious, but it wasn't. In that time, we built a fully functioning auction site. Jay Leno donated his motorcycles, and Bo Derek donated her bathing suits. By focusing relentlessly on execution and unleashing the potential of the team and the community, we raised $25 million.

Here are tools that I use to help drive an execution culture:

- **Clearly set cultural norms and standards about what you're trying to achieve.** I always made it clear we were after excellent performance and that we wanted to set aggressive goals. I didn't expect us to meet every goal, so I would give 100% credit for 80% of key goals made. It is also crucial to clearly articulate the definition of success for any given goal, and achieve alignment on these definitions with your team.
- **Calibrate teams on what great looks like.** "Great" should not be defined as what you think it looks like, but what the world thinks is great. Maybe it's graded as an "A," but you have to ask, is it an A in elementary school or an A in grad school? Too often, we celebrate greatness as getting better instead of being great on the world stage. If you are not vectored toward how the world sees greatness, it will just be okay—but not friggin' phenomenal. (You want friggin' phenomenal!)
- **Make sure everyone knows that identifying problems is a good thing, and that issues get resolved quickly.** I always set a standard that any big issue had to get owned and on a path to resolution quickly, ideally within twenty-four hours. I set high standards for myself on responding and troubleshooting, as I never want to be a blocker on critical path items.
- **Articulate clear ownership for every major task.** Ensure that the biggest tasks are appropriately resourced. You always have to know whose back to pat and whose butt to kick.
- **Implement forcing functions (e.g., 1:1s, project reviews, and weekly status updates) to ensure that things stay on track.** These are agreements on what you are going to do by when. Also schedule "deep dives" to ensure that work is on track and meets or exceeds the quality your company expects.

- **Keep teams as nimble and small as possible.** Even in big companies, keep the actual teams doing the work small. Build mechanisms to ensure that if any problems arise, they get escalated quickly. Pay attention to the whole team and stop by to see how they are doing. In addition to making sure they know the importance of what they are doing, make sure they know how much you believe they will do it.
- **Have teams and leaders grade projects and outcomes in a transparent fashion.** One of the best ways to set a culture of excellence is to have your own teams become tougher graders on themselves than you are. If every significant effort is realistically graded against the original goals with full transparency, good things happen. When things don't go well, explore why with an air of wonder and a commitment to improve.

Once a team has learned how to be a high-performing execution machine, you will have created an amazing asset. Now all you have to do is ensure you deploy it on the right strategies!

All the best,

Maynard

WHEN YOU NEED TO FOCUS ON WHAT'S IMPORTANT

Dear Founder,

Every day your inbox is flooded with new emails, your team approaches you for approvals, and your customers are requesting all sorts of new features. There's so much incoming, it's hard to get to all of it. It's hard to focus on what matters most.

A few years ago, when asked to write about a productivity hack, I wrote, "Why I don't 'do' coffee," and shared about how although I enjoy (decaf) coffee and stimulating conversation as much as anyone, I turn down these invitations in almost all cases.

I received a bit of backlash in the comments section, but I didn't mean to come off as aloof. It's just that I found that all of these meetings were an enormous time vortex because it was always a bigger commitment than a thirty- or sixty-minute meeting. Both parties have to travel to get there, and often someone is late. The hack I came up with—to connect via email instead of in-person meetings—helps me reach a far greater number of people and saves a lot of time that I can instead direct to my highest priorities.

All of us face so many demands and must constantly come up with hacks to save time. I've always tried to manage my time a certain way, but I never had a way to articulate it correctly until I read *The 7 Habits of Highly Effective People* by Stephen Covey. His Time Management Matrix helped me understand what was important and what wasn't—and how to focus on the things that matter.

Covey's framework delineates the things that matter today, things that may matter in the future, things that don't have a lasting impact, or things that don't matter at all. This matrix clearly revealed that the efforts that merited the most focus were those that were important—but not urgent (Quadrant 2).

Remember, Quadrant 2 takes deep introspection. It requires investing in what's most important. This includes your health. If you

STEPHEN COVEY'S TIME MANAGEMENT MATRIX **(with our own examples)**		
	Urgent	***Not Urgent***
Important	**Quadrant 1** • Site outages • Missing a quarter • Co-founder leaving • PR crises • Other "fire fighting" scenarios	**Quadrant 2** • Strategic planning • Painting a vision • Alignment • Communication • Inspiring the team • Delegation • Taking care of your health
Not Important	**Quadrant 3** • Unnecessary phone calls • Emails from people you don't know • Many social network updates • Any distractions that interrupt your daily flow and can be dealt with later	**Quadrant 4** • Any time wasters • Getting distracted by the startup "scene" (some parties and conferences) • Meeting everyone who requests time on your calendar • Micromanaging everything • Blindly following what everyone else is doing

do not take care of yourself, you will not have a productive life. I firmly believe that if you are able to do the Quadrant 2 activities that you need to do for your company and for your family, everything else will be beautiful. But neglect Quadrant 2, and you put your company, your family, and yourself at risk.

I think we all find that it's easiest to focus on what happens in the moment—especially when there is a crisis or deadline. Too often we mistakenly concern ourselves with stopping the bleeding, and we don't determine where the bleeding is coming from so we can stop it from happening again.

Of course, we must focus on what happens in Quadrant 1—companies can never succeed if they aren't diligently putting out fires and working on fire prevention. Yet, Quadrant 2—the not urgent, but important, space where all wise planning takes place—is where magic happens.

CEOs must learn how to turn chaos into order, so their companies can look like well-oiled machines. So, how do you separate signal from noise, and focus on what matters?

- Steal time from the "urgent and not important" Quadrant 3. Don't take telephone calls from someone you don't know.
- Don't plan or attend unnecessary meetings, which could fall into Quadrant 4. Build culture to make everyone else feel ownership of time that's wasted.
- Don't focus at all on Quadrant 4. Delegate—or remove—inconsequential tasks.
- Carve out Quadrant 2 time every week—make it a priority on your calendar and honor it. If you don't, no one else will; they will drag you back into 1, 3, or 4.
- Take time to reflect every week on how you spent your time and whether you spent enough time in Quadrant 2. I promise you that the more you are able to spend there, the less time will be needed in Quadrant 1. (Always be minimizing 3 and 4.)
- If you spend time on what must be accomplished every week, and review that daily, you will find that you stay more focused on the big goals instead of making everyone happy on things that don't matter.

One of the key skills for any leader to master is understanding what matters and what doesn't. We all have only so much time in the world, so it's best to spend it on things that are impactful.

All the best,

Maynard

WHEN YOU ARE FACED WITH A BET-THE-COMPANY DECISION

Dear Founder,

When you are faced with a true "bet-the-company" decision, it is my hope that you are looking at an opportunity to dramatically increase your growth and impact on the world.

There are times when things aren't going so well and you have to decide whether to sell, merge, or shut down the business. I don't see these as true "bet-the-company" decisions, so much as I do the outcomes of failed strategy or execution. (There are so many possible reasons why you may have reached this critical point: the market wasn't there yet, the idea didn't resonate, the team didn't execute, etc.)

In this letter, I focus on the offensive (not defensive) case for these types of decisions. This can be a dramatic shift in strategy; for example, think about Apple going after the phone market or Amazon launching AWS. It can also be a transformational acquisition such as PayPal for eBay or Whole Foods for Amazon. Just recently, Gilead Sciences announced an $11.9B acquisition of Kite Pharma in order to enter into cell therapy for cancer. Not all big bets are necessarily "bet-the-company" decisions, however. For example, in 2016, Visa completed a $20B acquisition of Visa Europe. While this was certainly a massive acquisition, Visa's purchase of Visa Europe was a restoration of what had been in place before Visa went public in 2008.

I had experience with one merger at Bay Networks that distracted us from what we should have been focused on—competing with Cisco. Being so focused on the merger took our attention away from innovating, which enabled Cisco to capture the switch market, and resulted in the sale of our company to Nortel. I had another situation where AOL was very interested in buying eBay, but decided instead to merge with Time Warner. (In theory that made sense: Time Warner would get tens of millions of new subscribers and AOL would gain access to a cable network and content. However, it didn't pan out and a visionary idea is now known as the "worst merger in history.")

Flops like that can give anyone pause, but sometimes, the big bets you *didn't* make were some of your biggest mistakes. Yahoo! had an offer on the table to buy Facebook in the mid-2000s. They had verbal approval at $1B but then Yahoo! continued to negotiate the price down. The deal fell apart.

When you are exploring how a deal can go wrong, I often imagine a big ship in the water. If we get hit by a torpedo (meaning the deal is going horribly wrong), does the torpedo hit us above the waterline, which means that we will survive, but have some patching and discomfort, or does it hit below the waterline where in all likelihood we may sink the whole company?

To try to figure out how this may go down, I advocate having a "white hat" and "black hat" present their cases to the board. Too often, all you have are white hat folks who are advocates for the deal. The black hat critics can be very valuable in considering the "parade of horribles" that can occur.

Another way to assess whether or not a "bet-the-company" decision is worthy of pursuing requires examining where the idea came from and who will be accountable for driving the implementation and results. Let me give you an example of what I mean and why it's important. One of our breakout companies is doing very well. On the current path, it will likely have a very meaningful (and life-changing for the CEO) outcome if the team keeps executing. They are seeing more competition, though, which increases risk. As a result, an idea has surfaced from investors about a significant merger. It could result in a huge and differentiated business—or it could result in failure. The CEO is smart and scrappy, but he is working very hard to grow his current business, let alone take on an entirely new business (and geography). Making this decision would likely mean a change in leadership over the whole enterprise.

My advice in this case: Don't do it. The CEO and founder aren't bought into the idea, it is high risk, and it truly could bet the company. The people driving the idea are not the ones who would be on the hook to pull it off, which is a problem. Right now the founding team is creating something very special with what they have; they should put all attention on capturing that. It is important to note that doing successful M&A is hard, and most companies are lucky to have 50% success with their acquisitions

Here's the logic I use to when making a "bet-the-company" decision:

- If it goes well and achieves everything you hope (understanding that it generally won't), what do you have?
- If it fails miserably, what have you lost and what impact does it have on the core business?
- Who is driving the strategy and how much passion do they have around it?
- What degree of confidence do you have that you can pull this off?
- Do you have dedicated resources to make this happen?

I think most decisions, even big ones, are not truly "bet-the-company" decisions. However, if you are faced with one, go slowly, refer to this list, and choose wisely.

All the best,

Maynard

WHEN YOU NEED TO GO FROM GOOD TO GREAT

Dear Founder,

Congratulations on doing well! Building a successful company from nothing is amazingly hard work. And you've done that—that's good. But now it's time to become great.

I've been most inspired by teams that are always seeking to become the best in the world at what they do. I find that the teams that achieve this end up being the most fun to be around, AND they deliver the most value.

There were a couple of times when teams I worked with got so great that they didn't know that what they were doing was seen by many as impossible. When I was working as a network director at Quantum, we had a pressing deadline to get long-distance circuits and technology infrastructure into new factories that were coming online. Not one telecom vendor said they could meet this deadline. Not being able to get the factories ready in short order would have delayed everything, costing us a considerable amount of money and damaging my reputation.

Rather than accept their refusals, I called a meeting with the vendor representatives to address the situation. I explained that the suppliers who were willing to find a way to work with us would build a long and profitable partnership with our company. I then challenged the vendors to find a way to help us. All it took was for one rep to raise his hand and say he could do it. The others followed, all committing to find a way to make an exception. We delivered the project on time, and my team started their journey of going from good to great.

Across our portfolio companies, we sometimes observe founders who confuse good with great, and for people who may not have seen greatness up close, it can be really hard to tell the difference. Many milestones are objectively good—large infusions of capital from venerable VCs, landing a marquis customer, hitting a hundred employees. And when you're a startup, these milestones will always look like progress from where you were a year ago. However, are you still doing great when you take a wider view of the ecosystem? What are the best in the world doing over that same period of time?

How can you get to great? Five strategies you should always implement:

1. **Understand what great looks like.** Think about telling an audience of a hundred people what you want to do. If they are not amazed, you're not aiming high enough. We all need to be looking at who is bold and audacious. Who is the best in the world, and what are they doing?

   Unfortunately, I have observed that most people manage to the mean, or compare themselves to what they did last month, rather than what the best in the world do. At eBay, when I took over customer support, the team walked me through what they were doing and how well it was going. "That's great, I think it's an 'A,' but don't know if it's an A in elementary school or in graduate school," I said. To figure that out, we looked outside to see what others were doing and built benchmarks. We found that each customer support representative was processing three to four emails an hour. The industry standard was fifteen. Once we knew how far behind we were, we set a new target, built a plan, and executed.

   People are naturally resistant to change. Internally and externally, I often find people say that something "can't be done." Generally, I find this answer results from a lack of effort, or a lack of imagination. If you can get your team to prove themselves wrong, they'll have done the impossible.
2. **Be on a constant quest to improve.** I recently returned from a three-day off-site with the top four hundred execu-

tives at Salesforce. We sat in a conference room in Hawaii diving into our plans and progress. While people were pleased with our progress (and there was certainly plenty to be pleased about), we spent a lot of time reflecting on what we could do better and faster. One reason Salesforce remains a great company is because it always wants to be better.

Do you always strive to deliver more? Ask the following questions:

- Who do I admire who is facing analogous challenges, and why? What do they do?
- What is achievable and by when? What is the highest we could aim for and hit? Always aim high, but know that if you have unreasonable expectations, you can burn out your team. Demanding too much can erode their trust not only in you, but more damningly, in themselves, too.

3. **Be very clear on the opportunity and what you are intending to achieve—and don't let anything get in the way.** When I was at eBay, we had a very talented executive team. We knew we had something special, and we all strove to hold each other accountable and to ensure that the company achieved its destiny. How can you set yourselves up for success?

- Give your team the tools they need for success (not only budget dollars and resources, but helpful forcing functions, check-ins, access to executives, escalation rights, and practices that set them up for success). Work every day to take all the excuses away on why something can't be done.
- Align the team so that they can make decisions quickly.

At Bay Networks, when we were working on a really fast Enterprise Resource Planning (ERP) implementation, people weren't making decisions quickly. To address the lag we were seeing, we introduced a twenty-four-hour rule where any problem had to get solved within twenty-four hours or it would escalate to me and the steering committee for rapid resolution. That project ultimately succeeded, and even earned a Computerworld Smithsonian Award nomination as one of the best technology implementations in the country that year.

4. **Do not hold your company back.** We had one founder in the portfolio who was at the crossroads of good and great. After years of middling results, he finally pivoted and tapped into massive customer demand. Eventually, he grew pent-up demand for sellers who wanted to use his service, but he was holding them at bay because he couldn't accommodate their supply. The business was continuing to grow like gangbusters, but *it could have been growing even faster.* At eBay, we ran into a bottleneck, too, where we once had a ninety-day window where we refused to add new users, because we couldn't add them and keep the site up. Over that time, the company still grew and made money, but we were selling ourselves short of greatness.
5. **Inspire others to greatness.** As a manager, this requires that we walk a fine line. I'm a perfectionist, so if I told people the full extent of what I really thought, I would probably leave them in a puddle most days. Instead, I've learned to inspire people and to help them extend their vision to become better and bolder. It's your job to instill confidence in your people and have them aspire to greatness on their own. That magic happens when you inculcate this philosophy into your teams.

Too many people aim too low. They feel satisfied with themselves when they are getting better, but they are not striving to be best in the world. I often see teams get excited when things get better. They should feel pleased with this progress, but they haven't reached high enough. The result? They settle for good, not great. Good is not good enough. Go for greatness.

All the best,

Maynard

WHEN YOU NEED TO KNOW THAT ANYTHING IS POSSIBLE

Dear Founder,

It's awesome that you created a company and got funding. But now what? What's next?

Hopefully, your dream is to be a breakout. Everyone wants to be Mark Zuckerberg or Marc Benioff, but for every thousand companies started, only half will survive and only a small fraction of those will be successful enough to be considered a breakout. It's like catching lightning in a bottle. So how do you do it?

While there's no formula, there are individual steps on the path to success that must be followed. It all starts with aiming high. What's high enough? It has to be amazing. If what you are thinking is not amazing, you need to step back and recalibrate and think bigger.

I had to learn this lesson in my own career. I started my career working as a security guard at IBM. I didn't know what the future held, and truthfully, I had no idea how amazing my future could be. My worldview of what was possible for me to achieve in my career was somewhat narrow. My biggest dream at that time was to become an IBM manager and own a home. While that was a big step up from where I was, I wasn't aiming high enough.

I always believed I was capable of achieving anything, I just didn't think the world would let me, given my background and some of the choices I made. I think I understood that I always had to better myself, and I knew I could, but I doubted whether the system would see my unique capabilities, as I took a very nontraditional route. I was, in the words of one executive who mentored me, "an acquired taste."

I had an unconventional childhood that was incongruous with the life I live today. My father died unexpectedly when I was seven years old. He didn't have life insurance and my mom had to go back to work to support five kids. We lost the air conditioner, hot water, and TV—and we also lost the opportunity to dream about what could be as we were too caught up trying to get by. Things weren't easy in school, either. They wouldn't let me enroll in Cub Scouts if Mom didn't serve as a "den mother"—something she couldn't do because she worked. Since the football program cost money to join, I couldn't play on an organized team until junior high, when it was free. When I was in elementary school, people thought I had a speech problem and that I should be in special education. Always, I was the kid without any father, without any money.

Still, I had big dreams, and I worked hard and saw the results. I won awards in school and was an MVP in football and Little League. I thought I was going to play in the major leagues. My mom was so worried that my head would get too big, she sarcastically called me "hero" as a way keep my ego in check.

No one ever spoke to me about applying for scholarships or aiming to go to college. No one expected that I could be better than good—and that I could hustle my way to great. No one told me that there was such a thing as a breakout. I was only told that I would have to take care of myself when I graduated high school. That curtailed the possibilities. While both of my parents went to college, I was the first of my siblings to get a degree. For all of us, the options felt somewhat limited.

I wish we knew then that the options were boundless. I wish I knew that we could create opportunities for ourselves, that jobs could be exciting and fulfilling—and that we each have a role in building an extraordinary life. In working, I learned:

- One opportunity could beget another, and hard work—especially volunteering for the hard jobs no one else wanted—could yield stratospheric success.
- A lot of it is about jumping in the water. A pedigree, while a good stepping-stone, is not the only way to get where you

need to go. The only way to get where you need to go is to actually go for it: Show up, knock on the door, and then run through it.

- When you try and succeed, you'll see winning is fun—and addictive. You will want to do it over and over.
- But you can't ever become cocky. You have to learn how to win gracefully. Stay humble and live up to the hype about you.
- Remember, even if you are a breakout, it doesn't mean you will stay a breakout. You will always have to prove yourself, again and again. With successes, you will gain the perspective that what you once saw as a mountain was just a hill, and you will realize that you still have a ways to go to reach your peak. Always focus on the next range of mountains in front of you.

Although I cleaned up over the years, I never quite looked the part to get me in through the front door. However, I learned there were still giant opportunities even when you came in through the kitchen. After a decades-long career, I've come to understand that what society expects you to do is not all that you can do, or are going to do.

We are all capable of more than we think we are. Dream big, and execute bigger. If you are willing to dream and then work hard and execute well, you can achieve more than you ever imagined. I wish you clarity in what you want to achieve, the willpower to work hard to accomplish your dreams, and the satisfaction that comes from knowing you gave it your all.

All the best,

Maynard

WHEN YOU NEED TO SCALE

Dear Founder,

Companies are not static; they're either growing or shrinking. Moving in either direction is hard work (though it's a lot more fun to be growing).

If you're struggling to keep up with your company's success, this is a great problem. Congratulations on building something the world wants! Now, you need to determine how to get ahead of the curve, so you don't limit your company's trajectory.

Before we jump into solves, let's first add a little more color to growth issues. The more you grow, the more friction you introduce. Challenges get harder as you become more successful. Onboarding a new employee at a small startup is a lot of work, but what happens when there are fifty new people? Two hundred and fifty? Or, what about when you add your first international branches, and to date every employee has lived and worked in a single geography?

All of those changes are good things, but they are hard to do well. If you have a problem that didn't get fixed last quarter, it could get in the way of what's happening this quarter. You have to be relentless at getting better and better. You have to always figure out how to make everything easier. This letter is about making the hard easier.

One of the ways to navigate these scaling hurdles is to learn how to become more discerning. You need to understand which priorities are most important. As you grow, there will always be more items clamoring for your attention, and it's up to you to decide which of these are most important.

I recently had a difficult discussion with the CEO of one of our portfolio companies. I was concerned about where the company was, whereas the CEO was satisfied with how far it had already progressed. In a way, we were both right. The company was doing very well and there was much to be proud of. Still, I believed it could be growing much faster. The team had built something magical and it was now at a critical juncture where it was ready to take off. This seminal moment offered a very rare opportunity—and I knew that they had to seize it.

That meant a lot of heavy lifting. When it comes to scaling, there is always something to do. The company must fill positions quickly, onboard new hires successfully, get customers clamoring to the business, ensure everyone is fired up, and have the world understand how it is different.

While the CEO was looking backward—how far they had come—I was looking forward, to where I thought they could go. I saw that as ringing the bell at NASDAQ and making it as a public company. However, that requires infusing a certain rigor into the organization. In this case, it also meant solving challenges such as open spots, morale issues, and missed quarters that would hold the company back.

For a company to be successful, it must be growing and scaling. I always find it fascinating how people find "innovation" to be exciting (despite how routinely it fails to pay off), but react to words like "operational excellence" or "rigor" (which almost always correlate with better outcomes) with yawns. If you can figure out operational excellence, it will be massively great for your career and company. It's far easier than you think—if you focus on it.

There are many tools and methodologies to help you see what "great" looks like and help you get there. We used to tout Kanban, Key Performance Indicators (KPIs), and Objective and Key Results (OKRs). In programming, Agile Methodology has largely replaced the once-popular waterfall development approach. I personally use Capability Maturity Model (CMM), and Salesforce employs Marc Benioff's V2MOM methodology, both of which I've included below. Yet what I really want to impart is not one particular process, but the importance of implementing a process to drive predictability to your company's operations. You need to have some kind of external methodology that helps you look at the company, see where you are, and determine where you need to be.

When I walk into any situation, the first thing I do is assess it. All companies, no matter how new or how mature, go up or down the maturity model based on market conditions that are very fluid. All companies move throughout these different phases on their quest for success.

This is the way I measure a company's status:

Level 1. This is the disaster scenario. You didn't do what you said you would do and people are running around with their hair on fire (metaphorically). On any given day you can slip into Level 1—a meeting runs late, you miss your window to get to your next meeting, and you don't gain pertinent information. When things start to spiral out of control, take measures to correct the situation immediately.

Level 2. You didn't yet achieve what you set out to do, but you have a clear plan in place. The plan is credible, you know who owns which tasks and goals, but you're not effectively implementing the plan yet.

Level 3. You don't have a lot of crises at this point. Your organization's "say-to-do" ratio is close to one. You are predictable and reliable, but you are not achieving all the potential that you have. Your growth is healthy and your business is accommodating it well, but you need to build on this stability to gain momentum—and get ahead of the curve.

Level 4. You are operating efficiently. You are able to do more with less, and the feeling of winning is palpable. For example, when we got ahead of the scaling challenges at eBay, there was a palpable difference. Our community members were happier, most of us got more sleep and we all loved it so much we vowed to stay there. (I do find it interesting that the people who climbed from Level 1 or 2 to Level 4 never forget the climb and resolve never to go back. Team members who join at 4 don't always understand the pain involved in the transformation and this leads to teams getting complacent.)

Level 5. Your team can operate without you, and it's taking less time to get things done. You are now a resource for others. At this point, you are now able to chase new and additional opportunities. You have discovered the holy grail, where you are working on what matters most.

Remember, achieving success will mean having to continuously level up your company, and each division, over time. That's why it's so important to not just tread water and stay alive for today (Level 3), but to get ahead of the curve to prepare for tomorrow (Level 4). Also important to note: None of this framework is static. You can be doing a Level 5 activity (a great project that will be important tomorrow), while living in a Level 3 world (where you are stable, but not yet secure for the future). And, you can have a Level 1 issue (losing a key employee) limit you and take time and cycles from where you want to be.

When I joined eBay the company was at Level 1. I was brought in as Mr. Fix It. They said things weren't working. That's a euphemism for not scaling. My task was to take chaos and turn it into order. Here's how we did it and a simple road map that you can follow:

- First, talk about what success look like.
- Decide what's important and develop metrics on the key things that matter.
- Implement forcing functions.
- Have timely communication, where issues are addressed in minutes or hours, not days or weeks.
- Escalate problems.
- Understand that it's not about what information you discover, but what you do with it. (Always ask, "What do we know now and what do we change?")

One of the simplest and the best tools I've encountered to help scale is the V2MOM process that Marc Benioff pioneered and still uses successfully at Salesforce, one of the most innovative and fastest-growing companies in the world.

V2MOM has been used to guide every decision at Salesforce—from those that were made in 1999 when the company started, to the decisions it makes today. The best part is that the same structure works for every phase in the life cycle of an organization. You can write one as a business plan, and the same construct is effective for outlining the annual goals of a public company. The same tool can also cascade throughout the organization. At Salesforce, everyone has a V2MOM, which maps back to the corporate V2MOM so everyone knows what they are doing and how their work furthers the company's larger goals. It's a great process that has enabled the company to be highly introspective and transparent, hold itself to a high standard, and fix mistakes fast.

The V2MOM is simple; I've included a template for it here.

VISION (Have a dream. What do you want?):

____

____

VALUES (What's important about it?):

____

____

METHODS (How do you get it?):

____

____

OBSTACLES (What might stand in the way?):

____

____

MEASURES (How will you know when you have it?):

____

____

As companies achieve success, they inevitably see new challenges and frustrations, which is completely natural. There will always be new situations so build rigor around you—to self-assess, and to know where you are going and what it will look like when you get there. And as hard as scaling is, if you plan to make your company successful, there's simply no alternative. Good luck!

All the best,

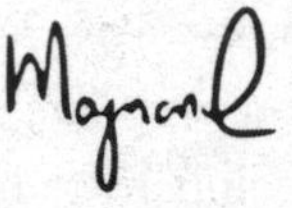

Maynard

WHEN YOU WANT TO RUN AN EFFECTIVE BOARD MEETING

Dear Founder,

As someone who has sat through hundreds and hundreds of board meetings over the decades, my sarcastic answer on how you can run an effective board meeting is simple: run an effective company. If your company is meeting or exceeding expectations, almost all board meetings—even when sloppily run—are good.

The problem is that too often this is not the case. With most companies, growth is not always up and to the right, and therefore you want and need board members helping you all along the way. That means the pressure is on: You'll need to run your meetings exceptionally well.

It's important to point out that board members generally get to know you and experience your leadership skills mostly through board meetings, so they may (rightly or wrongly) extrapolate how you perform in other areas of your company based on how you perform in the boardroom.

A successful meeting starts with alignment between the board members and you. In the beginning, ideally these meetings can be like deep 1:1s with a little time carved out for legal formalities (e.g., approving, stock, and other formalities that need to be discussed). These meetings will go much more smoothly if you have understanding and agreement in advance—on frequency and length of meetings, agenda, and management participation.

As you get bigger, these meetings become more formal and require an adjustment. As a side note, the longer you can stay small and intimate with your board, the better—but this is not possible forever. As you go through round after round of financing, you are often adding a board member at each round and changing the overall board dynamic.

When you are a big public company, you have lots of regulatory and compliance activity to contend with, and you will need special committees (such as audit, compensation, nominating, and governance to name a few), in addition to general board topics. Board and committee meetings at big companies are often two full-day events (or longer) and include a dinner as well. Themes and topics for board meetings are often baked in well in advance. For example, it may be determined that strategy will be covered in the July board meeting and the next year's budget will be approved in the January board meeting. Meetings and dates are scheduled at least a year, if not longer, in advance because it requires coordinating between many very overscheduled board members and advisers.

(If you are freaking out, now is the time to take a deep breath. The good news is that you are years away from that kind of setup, but I wanted you to understand that if you go public, that is where you are headed.)

In the meantime, it's important to note that your board will grow and that it will always require active management. A few simple rules to make things easier for everyone:

- Set up the meetings well in advance.
- Make sure board members know whether it is okay to attend remotely or not. (I just experienced a board meeting that the CEO changed to video at the last minute, and one of the board members had cut a European trip to make it back in person—oops! You don't ever want to do that.)
- Send out a proposed agenda a week or two in advance and solicit input for any topics the board wants to cover.
- Make sure all materials get out in advance (at least two days before the meeting). Board members are usually busy, but want to do a good job. When you don't give them time to do their jobs well, they get cranky.

- Leave time for an executive session with the full board, and with just outside board members.
- Save time at the end of the board meeting for board members to give you feedback.

All the best,

Maynard

WHEN YOU SHOULD PUT YOUR BOARD TO WORK

Dear Founder,

Congratulations! You've built a successful company. You now have a board. Hopefully you raised a few great rounds and picked up some incredible investors and phenomenal board members. Now what?

I would strongly suggest putting them to work. This is in addition to the normal board meeting routines where you are giving updates and they are providing advice and approvals. Keep in mind that this is probably your first CEO role while they likely have vast experience and have probably been a board member numerous times. That makes them an excellent resource.

- Solicit their advice on all kinds of matters, such as requesting examples of board decks, getting board agenda advice, inquiring about their style of preferred communication, asking what reporting they need for their firm, and more.
- If you are starting to ramp up go-to-market, solicit their help in opening doors to key prospects.
- When you are looking for key hires, invite them to suggest candidates. A word of advice here: If they give you recommendations, be sure to follow up on them. It can be irritating to a board member who responds to a request for help, only to have that ignored instead of acted on.
- Ask for their input on many key decisions, without abdicating the decision. Remember, board members (generally speaking) like to be part of the dialogue on big decisions as opposed to being told to vote on something that you've already made up your mind on.
- Whenever practical, be sure to recognize your board members for their contributions as well. At WIN, we often ad-

> vise our founders to send out periodic updates on their progress and recommend they call out investors who were helpful. This "gamifies" the process. (I know I always want the WIN team to be on the list of helpful investors!)

It is my hope that you not only raised the money you needed to grow your company, but that you also now have on the board a trusted adviser to help guide you. While I totally advocate putting your board to work, I also advocate that you do this in a manner that is respectful of their time.

All the best,

Maynard

WHEN YOU WANT TO AVOID NASTY SURPRISES

Dear Founder,

If you opened this letter you're probably looking for ways to avoid nasty surprises. I always say that problems don't get better with age. Therefore, I'm always on the lookout for potential issues and conflicts in the hope that we can surface them early—and fix them fast.

I wrote this letter to share the benefits of being proactive rather than reactive. Let me give you a real-life example of what I'm talking about. One time, at Yahoo! we had a long-scheduled board meeting. Unfortunately, it had never been communicated to several new board members. I had repeatedly asked about it, but the company wasn't sure it still wanted to have a meeting. Ultimately, it was necessary to hold the meeting in order to file our proxy by a certain time. While there was no choice about having the meeting, that didn't mean that it would be easy to ensure that all board members could attend. So, the scramble began to try and get the board together. Of course, by this time four of the thirteen members couldn't attend due to conflicts. I proactively reached out to all four, apologized for the churn (which is almost always avoidable and was in this case), explained why the meeting had to happen, and let them know I would be happy to represent them and their point of view in the meeting. One of the four hadn't heard anything about the meeting and was very suspicious, which then required my taking time to carefully explain everything to alleviate the concerns. Personally contacting them was pivotal. If we had conducted the meeting without proactively reaching out first, I'm certain there would have been much more fear and that it would have ignited trust issues.

Allow me to share another recent example of solving an issue before it became a problem: One of my WIN Labs founders was sending me weekly status updates (I did not force him to do this, but I appreciate that he does it). I had been away on vacation and I didn't get one. The next week I didn't receive one, either. I proactively asked him where his status was and he said, "I sent it to you." I was with him, so we went to my email to check and I confirmed I definitely hadn't received it. We discovered that he was sending the updates to a WIN alias that I wasn't on. Had I not checked up, he would have continued sending these weekly reports assuming I was getting them and probably wondering why I hadn't commented on any of his communications. And I would have continued to miss all the great information he was sharing in his weekly statuses. While this would not have been the end of the world, if left unchecked, it could have led to a schism between investor and founder. Instead, we solved it when it was simply a miscommunication.

In other letters, I've talked about productivity and forcing functions. Productivity is all about getting way more done than the average person—and we all know nasty surprises often derail you from great productivity. Forcing functions (including 1:1s and status reviews) help surface problems early and provide you with an opportunity to immediately address any issues that arise, making them useful tools to help increase productivity.

Yet it's not enough to assign tasks and integrate forcing functions. There are soft skills that matter here, too. I make a habit of spending time focused on getting to know most of the key people on every project. This includes checking in with them frequently and observing body language to get a deeper sense of what else may be happening. It also includes observing the chemistry of the team. I learned the value of observation while I was at eBay and sat in a cubicle. Initially I hated sitting in a cube! I had been in an office for years and had often retreated to my office to hide when things got tough. Now, everything was out in the open. When there was tension, it was palpable. And that made it easier to intuit what was going on. With that, something amazing happened—issues were resolved much faster because we didn't want to live with these problems anymore.

Some thoughts on how to solve problems early, or even prevent them from happening:

- **Be respectful of each other's time.** Communicate early what you need and by when. Obtain a commitment to have people get back to you when needed. If you're always in crisis mode and changing meetings and times, you are causing massive churn for others on your team. This, in turn, can lead to massive churn for their teams.
- **Teach your team that identifying problems should be encouraged and that early warnings are also appreciated.** It's much harder to solve problems when you are out of time to do so. Of course, you need to also teach your team how to come up with solutions on its own as well.
- **Check in frequently on the things you care the most about.** Have formal check-ins and frequent 1:1s, as well as informal and impromptu check-ins.
- **Pay attention to all the signals that exist.** I've often had to probe deeply with somebody whose behavior, attitude, or patterns have changed, and in doing so I've discovered early signs of a problem. Look out for changes in cadence around communication and listen to what other people are saying. As they say, where there's smoke, there's fire.
- **Always do the postmortem.** When you end up with a problem that could have been solved earlier, take the time to debrief the team on how to do better next time. Set expectations on what's expected when similar situations arise.

I promise you that if you inculcate the practice of surfacing problems early and fixing them fast, your job as CEO will become far easier AND more fun!

All the best,

Maynard

P.S. If you are receiving this too late and you already have a nasty problem, see the "When you have a crisis" letter in the next chapter!

8

Organizational Challenges

WHEN YOU HAVE A CRISIS

Dear Founder,

So, you've found yourself in a crisis. It's never fun to have something unexpected bomb-in on your plans and day, but it happens to all of us and it happens often. How you deal with these issues is what matters. Will you let a crisis utterly derail you and your business, or will it make you stronger and better?

Whether it happened unexpectedly or it happened because you haven't managed something well, the imperative is to deal with it now before it becomes something bigger. My advice: overreact instead of underreact.

However, before we get into HOW to resolve it—which is most important here, and which I'll get into below—let's take a step back.

What's the magnitude?

First of all, let's determine: Do you REALLY have a crisis? Listen first. What's the crisp description of the problem? Now, how bad is it?

You need a way to categorize it. In other words, you need a way to measure the mess. At eBay, Meg Whitman and I would judge incoming issues on the Richter scale model, which gave us a quick, 1–10 scale to measure the seriousness of the issue. A "1" is the routine noise that happens every day, such as a user having a problem with their computer and not being able to log onto eBay. (That wasn't the end of the world and there wasn't much we could do.) A "9," for example, was when the site crashed due to a power outage and the backup didn't come on. Ask yourself: Is this a tremor that will pass, or is this a killer earthquake you can't recover from?

So, you've now assessed the seriousness, and let's say you have a big problem—a "6" or above on the Richter scale and a threat to the business. Time to get to work.

There's no time to waste.

If you put a frog in boiling water, it will quickly jump out. But if you put it in and heat the water slowly, it will stay there—and cook. Do not stay in hot water for long.

I often say that problems don't get better with age. Too often, people choose to hide problems or let them sit, rather than addressing them when they're smaller. Remember the issue with the Tylenol cap? Or Intel's Pentium chip? Think about how differently Tesla responded to a seat belt malfunction. It recalled every car and managed the problem proactively. As Meg Whitman used to say to me, "Run into the fire!"

Deploy your resources.

It's time to get all hands on deck. The first thing to do is to sound the alarm to get immediate attention—and action. At eBay, we developed codes (Severity 1, Severity 2, etc.), which helped us immediately identify the scale of the problem and the response time. (A "Sev 1" would be dealt with immediately, while a "Sev 4" could be handled the next day.) We also incorporated terminology like "911s," which meant that every resource in the company could be pulled off of whatever they were doing to work on the current issue.

You'll be amazed at what people can accomplish when they come together to address a crisis. However, a word of caution: Use emergency status judiciously. It may be tempting to escalate future crises to "911" to get a faster response time, but don't. It will burn your team out fast.

Get the right people in place.

Talent is everything. When you are in crisis mode, you quickly get to see people at their best and at their worst. In the middle of a crisis, I learned that I was understaffed with the right talent. I decided that I needed to add several key executives ASAP to my team as direct reports, and I did this within weeks. I've also seen a few people who may have been a tad cranky, attitude-wise, save the day during a major incident. Make sure you have the best surgeons, firefighters, and problem solvers on board—and if you don't, get them there quickly.

Have a backup plan. And a backup for the backup.

Let's be honest: When a problem hits, you don't always know what's wrong, and you certainly don't always know how to fix it. Such was the case for me in early 2000 when several internet companies fell victim to denial-of-service attacks. We had to work with vendors, deploy patches, and collaborate with other tech companies and law enforcement to determine how to stop it.

I was always a fan of working on several possible solutions simultaneously, just in case we were wrong in our hypothesis. If you want to solve a problem fast, it's always better to develop many possible solutions in parallel than to serialize the process. Furthermore, always look two to four moves ahead so you have options. Keep asking yourself, *And if that doesn't work, then what?*

Swallow your pride.

It's not about hierarchy. The best answers can come from anywhere. Allow everyone to have a voice and contribute insights and questions throughout the process. What's most important is to solve the problems quickly and prevent their recurrence. Always ask yourself: *Are we getting better every day?* If not, make some changes.

Do everything possible to minimize impact for customers.

I reference eBay a lot, probably because it was crisis central. When I started, we used drives from a big vendor and when they crashed, our entire site crashed. The vendor told me that we were trying to recover "too fast" and if we just let them recycle for twenty minutes, everything would be fine. Who has twenty minutes on the internet?

We agreed that the current situation was unsustainable, and the vendor went to work on a firmware solution. However, we needed a proactive interim strategy. For twenty-four hours a day, we kept people watching for the warning that would flash before a crash. Once it went, they would take the disk out of service before a crash happened. It was a high-intensity solution that required a lot of resources, but until it was automated with a bug-free software fix, we had to do everything within our power to reduce how customers were affected.

Most executives would not ask the vendor to do what I did, but it was critical to find a solution that didn't impact the customer—even if it was ugly for someone else. Sometimes you have to be a barbarian in wartime.

Communicate with everyone (i.e., the board, your team, customers).

Have your board and your management on high alert and make sure they're present until permanent solutions are in place. Do not hide from anyone.

At eBay, I wrote personal updates on issues to the management team and every week gave status reports on what went well and what didn't. Make it one of your action items. Also, get every executive's mobile number and the personal cell phone numbers of every vendor so you can mobilize resources as quickly as possible.

Remember, you're not just solving for the problem with your team in a silo; customers are involved. Someone has to notify them and calm them down. Silence is not a good thing at this stage. Here's how to take action during a crisis:

- Tell the truth.
- Tell them the next steps.
- Tell them when you will update them again.

You'll need to have a process in place to communicate. Who's managing communications to employees, to customers, to the press? (Hint: It shouldn't be the surgeon in the operating room.)

The world will always want you to do more. The best thing you can do to address this demand is to create a culture of transparency and accountability. If we had a problem at eBay, we always communicated it to our community. Be careful about what you say. Be truthful, but keep in mind that often when you think you know what is going to happen or what is causing the issue, it may turn out to be something else entirely. At eBay, and later at Salesforce, a "trust site" and dashboard were built, giving full transparency into what was happening on the site to let people know what was going on in real time.

Postmortems are essential.

Never waste a crisis. It's an opportunity to make things better. Once the problem is solved, figuring out what went wrong (Was it an execution issue, a vendor or product issue, a software bug, an external event, etc.?), and how to ensure it won't return, is essential. Remember, great companies have to be world class at dealing with crises, but they aspire to be even better at avoiding crises in the first place. (You'll need to master BOTH. If you're in a crisis it's too late to worry about prevention, so you better be great at getting out of trouble!)

From now on, plan for crises in advance.

Ideally, you want to be deploying a playbook rather than developing a playbook. Most often, founders don't do this in advance and then have to develop processes while in battle—that's much harder. At eBay, we built plans and put processes in place that anticipated problems. There was 24/7 coverage and people were assigned to be on call in order to respond quickly to any issues. This proactive approach saved us time in the most critical moments. For example, when we learned that hours after 9/11, people were putting debris from the World Trade Center for sale on the site (a "6" on the Richter scale), we knew how to respond because we had a policy in place that detailed that we would not profit from disaster. Thanks to our policies, we were able to react immediately and take it down.

At eBay, we got so good at fire prevention and firefighting that we were no longer battling them all the time. Things became calm—and then that became an issue.

"We used to be so important," someone on the team said to me. "Now Meg doesn't come by every night to see how we're doing."

"That's how it's supposed to be," I told them.

You, too, will have peaceful moments when things are going well again. Enjoy those for a moment and then use that time to invest in making your business better.

All the best,

Maynard

WHEN YOU'VE JUST MISSED YOUR QUARTER

Dear Founder,

I can only imagine how you're feeling. I have a lot of sympathy. As a perfectionist myself, it kills me when I don't deliver on what I committed to do.

Let's stop for a moment here and appreciate the discomfort you're feeling right now. It's painful. (If you are not feeling uncomfortable, that's a big problem.) Let's use this knowledge to harden your resolve so you'll prevent this unpleasant situation from reoccurring.

Now, we have to think about why this has happened. To determine that, I have some questions for you:

- When did you start to *think* you might miss the quarter? When were you *certain*?
- Did you communicate this concern? Did you message anything in advance, or did you wait, hoping for a miracle?

  - Boards don't do well with surprises. And, like with all problems, bad news doesn't get better with age.
  - If this comes as a surprise to the board, how big of a surprise is it? Where would it fall on the Richter scale?
  - Remember, when things don't go well, people are looking for you to step up and lead in a bigger way.
  - How you handle sharing bad news is a great way to instill more confidence in your leadership.

- What was the business issue that caused the problem? (Answer these questions clearly and definitively to understand why. Own it. Do not be defensive.)

- Was your planning flawed? Were your goals unrealistic?
- Was your execution flawed? If you underexecuted, at what phase did this happen (e.g., sales, technology development, marketing, etc.)?
- Was the product flawed?
- Did the market for the product or service tank?

- How bad is the situation? Is it a cold, is it the flu, or is it something more serious that could be terminal?

    - If it's a cold: Find a way to recover quickly and still make the year. The quarter is gone, but don't give it up yet. Work harder to get back on track. Overdeliver for the next quarter and try to make up for the miss.
    - If it's the flu: You probably won't make the year and your next round may be at a lower valuation than hoped, but you may still be on a good long-term trajectory if you put the right recovery plans in place and execute on them.
    - If it's a serious illness: There will be lots of angst and discord in the boardroom. If you don't have a lot of cash in the bank and you need to raise money, it will likely result in a down round with onerous terms. It's not pleasant. This often leads to leadership changes. You can escape from near-death experiences, though. I joined eBay under such circumstances. The company had just missed its quarter after losing significant revenue during an outage. It was 1999 and the company lost $10 billion in market cap. It was bad, but it wasn't terminal (mostly because there was no alternative to eBay at that time). Customers needed us to list their items and we had to figure out how to keep up with the demand in order to survive. I know firsthand that you can have a miss and still pull through, but you need to turn things around fast or you won't be around much longer.

    - If it's terminal: Work on minimizing your cash burn, get acquired or acqui-hired if you can, and return cash to investors.

- How can *you* get better? The board and the people at the company want to know how this affected you.
    - Did this defeat you? Or, did it harden your resolve?
    - Do you know what to do next?
    - Are you doing this with urgency—better, faster, and stronger than ever?

- If the miss doesn't have dire near-term implications for your company, then it's important to not let this change your belief in your company. Don't let this change the trajectory of *hope* for the company.
    - Set aggressive goals. It's important.
    - Be transparent about where you fell short and be positive about the momentum that you do have.
    - Don't become so conservative that you miss the opportunity you're striving for. Mediocrity is the worst place you can be.

At eBay, we used to say, "It doesn't matter what happened last quarter. The most important thing is to get back on track." You have to understand what went wrong, learn from it, do something differently, communicate more, and not give up. Lead through this. Leadership is about giving hope—and then delivering on it.

All the best,

Maynard

WHEN YOU NEED TO SOLVE CROSS-FUNCTIONAL FRICTION

Dear Founder,

Well, it appears that you must be having some success in your company. Your team has evolved from a group that was very cohesive and aligned every day, to one that is big enough to have different agendas and focuses. So, congratulations on your successful growth! Now, let's dive into what's going on (and determine how to help fix it).

First, it's important to realize that this friction you are experiencing is a natural state. Unfortunately, we don't automatically embrace and welcome people who are different from us. For example, engineers don't always intrinsically think salespeople are as important as they are. Also, everyone has their own work to do and when a new function or capability arises in the company, it generally brings new demands. Some people find these new demands threatening.

When you were first coding and building your product, you probably didn't have many interruptions from the sales and marketing teams inquiring how to help differentiate your product or suggesting new features. Now things are different. Everyone is hired to do a job and is needed, but as a company gets larger, the jobs increasingly require help from others. Most of the time, you only start interfacing with another group when you require something from them. Unfortunately, it's seldom the case that teams reach out to say, "I know you are working on something huge, how can I help you?"

That can be a problem. Too often we are unprepared for this next phase of business. Yet with a few changes in behavior, we can shift this scenario from something that causes stress to one that inspires seamless integration and growth. Here are some suggestions on how to tackle cross-functional friction:

- **Get peer alignment on goals.** I'm a fan of ensuring that everyone at the executive level gets input on one another's goals and on grading these goals later on. This also includes knowing what trumps what, and which goals matter most. When I first joined eBay, I had the head of development focused on shipping fast and furiously and I had the head of operations focused on availability. Needless to say, there was a lot of head-butting between the organizations. To resolve the strife, I had to intervene and decide what goal was most important. Eventually, I changed the goals of each team so that ops shared the delivery goals and product development shared the availability goals. When I added customer support to my team, we realized that we needed to add customer satisfaction to all the goals as well. Everything works much more smoothly—and pleasantly—when everyone is working toward the same goals.
- **Engage in broader communication.** Whatever you've been doing regarding communication is very likely not enough. Communication must be constant and it must reach everyone. Marissa Mayer at Yahoo! did an "FYI" for all employees every Friday. Yahoo! has had its struggles and challenges, but Marissa's willingness to stand up and face tough questions every week was a source of inspiration and calm for the company.
- **Implement decision-making guidelines.** What are the expectations for problem resolution? Who gets to make which decisions? I'm a fan of the RACI model (who is Responsible, who needs to Approve, who needs to be Consulted, and who needs to be Informed, which is detailed in another letter, "When you need to know who owns what"), but there are a number of methods you can use. What's most important is that you pick one and diligently stick to it.

- **Find ways to surface issues.** I ask everyone at WIN to submit things they need help on every week. In my 1:1s, I ask how things are going and why.
- **Celebrate the wins and give validation across the whole company.** When you see cross-functional behavior that is great, call it out and celebrate it. Our customer support team at eBay gave out "silver star awards" to those people who went above and beyond to help them out. There were lots of people at eBay who had the printed award up in their cube.

As you continue to grow and be successful, you'll need to find new and innovative ways to keep addressing cross-functional friction. Companies that know how to mitigate this (and realize that the enemy is not across the aisle, but outside the building), end up with far more capability and success—not to mention, the people at these companies have a lot more fun.

All the best,

Maynard

WHEN YOU NEED TO ASSERT THE CHARACTER OF YOUR COMPANY

Dear Founder,

There will be thousands and thousands of decisions and judgments made in the coming months and years at your company. Some decisions matter more than others. The types of decisions I am talking about here are ones that shape the bedrock of your company.

Some examples:

- When we see bad or illegal behavior, do we turn the other way, or do we address it head-on?
- What do we do when our service goes down (or does not meet expectations) in order to maintain our customers' trust?
- When our Glassdoor numbers are abysmal from current and former employees, do we just say they weren't a fit, or do we examine our behaviors?
- When our numbers for the quarter are not looking good, how do we talk about this to our board and to our team?

When I was at eBay, we had a board meeting scheduled and one of our directors, Howard Schultz (founder of Starbucks), arrived fresh off a trip to Germany and Poland. He was genuinely traumatized by what he had experienced when he visited the concentration camps, and specifically, the gas chambers. At the time, eBay sold Nazi memorabilia. Howard was opposed and adamant: He demanded that we stop selling these items immediately. There was a lot of back-and-forth on whether we should cease to sell these items as they weren't illegal. Howard didn't care about that; he said, "It's about the character of the company." He was right. When he eventually left the eBay board, we gave him a plaque with that motto.

I have a tremendous amount of respect for Howard and I learned a lot from him.

I have encountered several "character of the company" moments since, and I have always been comforted with how easy the decisions become when your value systems are clear.

So, while you are making all the decisions that you have to field, please keep an eye out for the ones that are about the "character of the company." In those cases I hope you will make your decision based on your core values. While we know we have to live to the letter of the law, our character and values require us to live to the spirit of the law, which is a higher standard.

All the best,

Maynard

WHEN THERE'S A CONFLICT OF INTEREST ON YOUR BOARD

Dear Founder,

Sometimes conflicts of interests within a board are very obvious. We recently had one at a Fortune 500 company, where we discovered one of our favorite candidates was currently on the board of another company. That's not normally an issue, but in this case that company and ours were in the midst of a massive legal battle. It was an easy decision—it wouldn't work unless the candidate quit the other board. Later, we had a similar situation, but this time the candidate was on the board at a subsidiary of the company, not the company itself. Could that be okay?

Sometimes conflicts of interest with board members are black and white issues. But most of the time, it's at least a thousand shades of gray. Having a balanced board is essential for success, but it's hard to build a board. You have to think carefully about the skills that are needed. For public companies, there are regulatory requirements for financial acumen. Industry and operating experience are also generally extremely valuable. Sometimes boards require international, technology, or sales expertise. Modern boards also value a diverse set of backgrounds, genders, races, and perspectives. Lastly, you have to solve for something more nuanced: chemistry. The best boards are independent, collegial, professional, and make the company better and shareholders wealthier.

The most challenging part of building your ideal board is that at any time, there are a limited number of potential candidates. Companies require the most talented individuals to fill these important seats. Often the best possible person for your business will have relevant experience in your industry—and that means they're likely to have conflicts. If the conflict is with a competitor, walk away. A direct competitor who can use your information for their gain is never worth the risk. However, in most cases, conflicts aren't so straightforward.

Sometimes you have to solve for something that was never anticipated to be an issue. An example: a number of years ago, I invested an immaterial amount in a small company creating software in a category that had been of no interest to Salesforce. Later, Salesforce became interested in acquiring the company. The solution: I stayed on the Salesforce board, but fully disclosed my small investment interest and recused myself from any discussion and decision-making about the acquisition.

Don't assume all perceived or potential conflicts present actual or unsolvable conflicts. You should not always write something off just because it could raise a perceived issue. Take time to investigate it thoroughly, and then make an informed decision. Process and disclosure can make a difference. When I was the CEO and chairman of LiveOps, LiveOps and Salesforce wanted to do business. But I was a board member at Salesforce. The contract amounts were ultimately not significant, but the situation could have presented potential issues. In this case, I disclosed my situation fully, the audit committee thoroughly vetted the transactions, and I recused myself from any decision-making on those transactions. Salesforce also disclosed those transactions to its shareholders.

However, understand that perception is reality. For example, two of the boards I sit on use Everwise, a company I co-founded. There were rules that helped us navigate this situation, which put limits on the amount of business Everwise can do with these companies. When shareholders or other board members perceive there to be a potential conflict—regardless of whether you agree—you must quickly address and vet it.

Be cognizant that companies and markets are fluid, and monitor continuously. Consider how there was very little overlap in 2000 between Apple and Google, and Google CEO Eric Schmidt served on both boards. However, some years later, things had changed substantially, and it became clear that they were both chasing a mobile strategy. Eric did the right thing and stepped off the Apple board. Businesses today change so rapidly, that what may not have been a conflict yesterday, can easily become one tomorrow. Reassess frequently.

Creating a balanced board requires a balancing act. While the best directors will have the necessary relevant expertise and zero conflicts, finding this magical board member is a little like finding a leprechaun. So, be open-minded, understand that some conflicts are more perceived than real, and then vet them thoroughly and continuously, and make changes as necessary.

All the best,

Maynard

WHEN YOUR BOARD SAYS THEY ARE REPLACING YOU AS CEO

Dear Founder,

There are bad days and then there are horrible days. This counts as a horrible day.

A difficult experience with one of the great entrepreneurs in our portfolio recently reminded me of this. I had just come from an emergency meeting for Yahoo! and walked into a scheduled meeting with the CEO and my WIN team. I apologized profusely for being late—this rarely happens—and explained I was having a tough time. I noticed that the CEO was very low energy, which isn't his normal M.O., and he said, "I bet we can argue about who's having the worse day."

He told me the board called the night before. They were replacing him as CEO. He had just met the new CEO, a very experienced startup CEO, that morning. He had been asked to stay on in a key strategy role. This founder was holding up amazingly well under the circumstances, but his angst was palpable.

What puzzled the founder most was that this had happened when he owned 50% of the company. Yet this happens way more often than founders think. Unless you are self-funding, there's always a risk that your job can be taken from you.

If you find yourself in this situation, think about the following:

- Is this a surprise?
- Assess whether this is recoverable or negotiable. Do you want to fight the decision? If yes, where does that lead?
- What does this mean for you and for your team? Do you message this as your decision and lead through it, or do you fight it and create a lot of emotion around your role? Are you still being asked to be involved in a big way?

- Will shareholders (and remember that you're also a key shareholder) end up better in the long run?
- Try to ease the transition. When I left LiveOps, I was willing to commit to staying as chairman for two years to help. I committed to the new CEO that I would help in a transition and I asked him how long he would like for me to stay. He said, "You can leave my first day." I didn't take this personally, as he had been warned by his former colleagues about having someone like me on the board and was concerned that I may overpower everyone else. Trying to retain control isn't my style, but he didn't know that. It's important that you offer what's right—despite how others might respond.
- Take some time. Figure things out. There's no way this will make sense to you immediately. Determine the insights and learnings you can take with you for the future.
- Be proud that you had the courage to start something from scratch. We are proud of the traction you've built.
- If you can't find an engaging role that you love and can get passionate about in the current company, don't grow bitter. Figure out round two. You're in control of the move you make next. Figure out what you're uniquely qualified to do and want to do. This situation was not in your hands, but the next one is.
- Finally, and I don't want to give any false hope, but we all know Silicon Valley "comeback" stories that involved greats like Steve Jobs returning to Apple, Larry Page returning to Google, and Jack Dorsey returning to Twitter. Nothing is impossible.

I'm very sorry you're going through this. You're amazing, and while this *is* a horrible day, rest assured there are better days ahead. You'll be smarter and stronger for having gone through this, and the experience will be reflected in what you achieve next.

All the best,

Maynard

PART IV

LEAVING A LEGACY

9

Building a Company to Last

WHEN YOU HAVE A BIG PAYDAY

Dear Founder,

Congratulations! Most of us never get to experience a big payday and many of us wish we could.

I decided to write a letter on dealing with sudden wealth because I have personally struggled with it as well as witnessed several colleagues who have had a difficult time managing this transition. I share this letter with you in hopes that you don't have to experience all the turbulence that we did.

In reality, as great as it all sounds, things often become even more complicated when you have to manage this new wealth. Hopefully, for most of us, while money was necessary, it was not the reason we chased our life's purpose.

First, it's important to understand what's what.

- You will pay a significant portion of your payday in taxes. Hopefully you were able to achieve most of your return as a capital gain. If not, if it's straight income, as much as 50% (based on your state) can be taxed.
- Too often people who come into money lose it quickly. This is not an unfortunate reality limited to NFL stars and lottery winners. It happens to entrepreneurs, too.
- Markets change. Probably, the most painful things I've experienced have been when market forces exert themselves—and not in a good way. When the "bubble" burst in the early 2000s, so did some of my net worth. The same thing happened again in 2008–2009. It's hard to think you have made your targeted or desired net worth, only to see it erode quite quickly.
- You need to find the right approach to navigate and manage newfound wealth. Many people work with financial advisers, but it's important to understand that these professionals

> aren't always working for you, though they say they are. I remember being excited when I was seeing my net worth grow due to my company doing well and some angel investment bets that had paid off. I had my money with a reputable big bank and soon I started noticing that there were lots of trades happening. I was paying hefty fees to my advisers for this kind of money management, yet the investments weren't doing very well. I switched advisers to a group that gets paid based on my net worth. When it grows, their fees grow and vice versa. Our interests are better aligned.

Suddenly gaining significant wealth can also introduce unexpected dynamics with family and friends. Ultimately my wife and I made decisions together, including making college help available to every blood relative and their offspring. We also focused on providing experiences—family reunions or special events, such as attending Super Bowl games. Our thinking is that we want them to have fun and enjoy these great times together, but we also want them to keep working hard to ignite their own success and reach their own destiny.

Once our immediate family was taken care of, we started a family foundation to give back to the world. We founded it in 2004 (thank you, eBay) and after a few years of figuring out where we could make the most impact, we settled on helping underprivileged children get a college education. It's been a lot of work to get it right, but also a source of joy and inspiration.

Congratulations on achieving a great return for all of your efforts and innovation! I hope you will find a way to celebrate this achievement and that you will be able to enjoy the impact of your effort for years—and hopefully generations—to come.

All the best,

Maynard

WHEN YOU NEED TO PLAN SUCCESSION

Dear Founder,

It's never too early to think about succession.

From the earliest days of getting started, you need to make sure you have the talent you need to achieve the destiny of your company. In the beginning, you have to think about succession planning as recruiting. We all know the bleak statistic—50% of hires don't work out. Additionally, though you may not be worried about people leaving your company, it is inevitable that this will happen. What if they decide they don't like you, or they find a job that pays five times what you can? Or they move away? Even if you have someone who seems great, you can't sit back and think you are all set for eternity. You need to always be planning who can step in so that you will not be left in the lurch.

This is a tricky balance: You must continue to challenge and groom your talent, and at the same time you need to explore and secure additional options in case it doesn't work out with your current team member. It may sound excessive, but the fact is it's impossible to spin up a team of the best talent from ground zero—this can only happen with constant investment in this effort. So how do you approach this delicate balance?

At all times you need to know the following:

In each position, how good is the talent you've got? If everything goes according to plan, will they be able to scale with you? Will they be able to grow so they can stay with you two years from now? How can you know that? Investigate what you *do* know. How are they doing today in delivering on one product? They are managing three people now; how is that going? Then, extrapolate out. What happens when they need to also manage customers? Based on how they manage three people, will they be able to manage thirty? Where do they break?

Who's on your bench? Even if someone is able to scale with you (and especially if they are flourishing, as this means that they will be promoted and then need to be replaced), you need to make sure that you have talent underneath them who can step in and do their job.

Who's best in class outside your company? You need to know who the best CMO is, who the best engineers are, who the best HR professionals are so you can develop relationships with them and try to tap them down the road. Marc Benioff is excellent at getting the best people on board even if there is not a position open—he's always looking to get people "on the bus" and he moves them to the right seat later. Similarly, Meg Whitman always made it her business to build a strong bench. Always ask yourself: *Is there somebody in the world who would be a dream candidate even if I can't have them in that exact role?*

So, what about you?

This is a difficult question. No one wants to think about getting replaced—it's a lot more fun to think you are indispensible—but you must plan for succession. The board should know who will take your place should anything happen that would change your leadership at the company. Public companies have that discussion at least once a year. It's not always easy, but it's always necessary.

You always want to recruit people better than you. And you always have to give people a chance. The fact is, a lot of people are willing to step up. They just need the opportunity and the mentorship. Give it to them.

All the best,

Maynard

WHEN YOU ARE THINKING ABOUT BUILDING A COMPANY TO LAST

Dear Founder,

I've written about going from an idea to relevance and then to scale. However, a truly successful business—a lasting one—doesn't stop there. Let's talk about going from scale to legacy.

Before doing this, let me first start with a disclaimer: If you are still truly a startup, you shouldn't be focused on legacy right now. Your focus must be on making your company relevant and then scaling. If you truly are already in scale-mode, then perhaps it is time to start thinking about how to create a company that will transcend generations—a company that will survive longer than your tenure. What does it take to create a company like GE or Ford or Apple—companies that last beyond their legendary founders and that impact generations of people?

Getting to scale is hard. Getting to legacy is almost impossible. The people who got your company off the ground, the people who scale it, and the people who help achieve legacy are rarely the same. Not only does it require a different skill set, the same people often will no longer be around.

We are seeing fewer and fewer companies span generations. Since 2000, more than half of the companies on the Fortune 500 list have disappeared as a result of mergers, acquisitions, or bankruptcies. Consider that in 1975 the life expectancy of one of those Fortune 500 companies was seventy-five years. Today, it's just fifteen according to John Hagel III at Deloitte's Center for the Edge.

Legacy is something I think about a lot these days, both in my personal career and when deciding which companies and founders to bet on. Yet this was not something I thought about early on in my career. And, in some ways, this was a mistake.

I think I got a taste of the power of legacy from IBM. The

founder, Thomas J. Watson, was memorialized—and I read every one of his management letters. IBM had a very firm culture and values.

When I first started working, I considered myself a member of the family at IBM, and my focus was on doing a good job so that I could stay. I didn't think about what I would do that would leave fingerprints on the company. As I moved up in my career, I felt that I was on a fast track through management roles, and I knew that I wouldn't stay long in any one job. I was thus set on getting things fixed quickly and leaving everything in good shape.

My first senior IT leadership job was at Quantum. People enjoyed working with me, but I made a mistake—I made the job about me, not about the company. As a result, when I left, a lot of people left with me. I was flattered, but with the benefit of hindsight I know that was not a win. Success is not about the individual; it's about the company. I took this lesson with me throughout the rest of my career. In my next posts at Bay Networks, eBay, and LiveOps, I was more interested in bettering the organization. As a result, when I left, people stayed at the company and worked toward making lasting contributions—contributions that would span long beyond any of our individual tenures. This is when I relearned that there's much greater fulfillment and power in working to build a legacy than in working on one's own career.

As a founder, you can't worry about being legendary when you are starting out. However, you should always be aware of your own impact on your company. Meg Whitman said, "When you are a founder, your fingerprints never leave." Indeed, HP is guided by Bill Hewlett and David Packard every day. This often happens in small and sometimes unexpected ways. Take Yahoo!'s legendary purple paint story. Jerry Yang sent Yahoo! co-founder David Filo out to buy gray paint and David mistakenly got purple instead. That set Yahoo!'s identity. To this day, they say, "We bleed purple."

When you are thinking about leaving a legacy, you are not thinking about yourself. Here's what you do have to think about:

- Have you codified the secret sauce that makes you special?
- Are your values inculcated firmly? Have you taught people how to modify them when needed?
- Do you have, at the ready, successors who can carry on the mission (and hopefully improve it)? The company should be able to continue on its merry way—and without any hiccups—without you.
- Embrace servant leadership. Put the cause ahead of your agenda and beliefs.
- Get out of the way, but be willing to insert yourself when legendary status is at risk. (Think Steve Jobs's reinsertion into Apple.)

It is absolutely amazing and incredible to be part of a legacy company that's reaching thousands to millions of people on a global scale. John Donahoe, the former CEO of eBay, used to talk about his humbling and inspiring opportunity to "steward" eBay for almost a decade of its journey. You always want to make a company better than it was when you joined. As you can see from the statistics about company life span, this is very hard work. However, the opportunity you have to create something that lasts makes it totally worth it!

All the best,

Maynard

A Final Note

If you've made it this far, I appreciate your taking the time to read all of these letters. They come from decades of dealing with gnarly situations and an unrelenting spirit that knows building a company to last is special and holy.

I had a blast codifying what I've learned into this book. I also know that there are many ways to solve even the most challenging conundrums. I'm still learning—and I'm still writing. If you have questions or ideas for new letters, send them to us at our site: maynardwebb.com.

I have a deep love and appreciation for the founders, CEOs, and executives who work tirelessly to build and grow companies. My wish is that this book helps you achieve your companies destiny and your dreams. It is a privilege to try to help you; I am here to serve you on your journey. It is a difficult—but infinitely worthwhile—one.

Acknowledgments

I am grateful to everyone involved in the Webb Investment Network journey.

Thank you to Mitch Kapor for inspiring me to do what I am called to do. I'm grateful to my co-founders, Michael Neril, Kevin Webb and Irene Webb, the entire WIN Team, as well as all of the founders and all of our affiliates. This book flowed naturally from our interactions.

I had an amazing time working with the WIN team on this project.

We couldn't have done this without Carlye Adler, my writing partner, who was as energized as I was by the endless amount of topics to cover. Thank you to Jonathan Pines, Jeremy Schneider, and Kevin Webb for supplementing my letters and for sharing their invaluable wisdom on the fundraising process in your own letters. Thank you Heidi Burns for making our community stronger and for the great feedback. The amazing Dena Porter is the powerhouse behind everything—designing systems to allow us to work efficiently and the force behind the digital edition of this project.

Many of our founders and affiliates were generous with their time and thoughts and I credit their feedback with encouraging us to publish this book more broadly. A special thank you to Mike Bergelson, Laura Mather, Arend Naylor, Masha Sedova, and Matt Tucker for reviewing letters and sharing your perspectives. Thank you to Pete Cittadini, Harsh Patel, Adam Goldstein, and Monty Kersten for contributing letters that generously share your hard-earned wisdom.

Thank you to Howard Schultz for graciously contributing a foreword for the book and for your collaboration and inspiration.

Many people shared their insights and reviewed these letters on multiple occasions, making them far stronger: Beth Axelrod, Cory DuBrowa, Dan Farber, Monica Langley, Lori Nishiura Mackenzie, Michael Ross, Kelly Mahon Tullier, Amy Weaver.

The fantastic team at LEWIS PR helped edit an early edition of this book and developed a plan to allow these letters to reach a broader audience of entrepreneurs. Miles Daniels thank you for your ideas around how to extend this project beyond what we originally anticipated.

I'm appreciative of literary agent Jim Levine for his belief in this project and for ensuring we collaborated with the perfect publishing partner. We are grateful to everyone at St. Martin's Press, especially George Witte, who instantly got the book and whose vision for it made it even better, and Sara Thwaite, who patiently and pleasantly shepherded us through the entire process.

I would like to thank my family. My mother, Helen, set an unbelievable example of how not to let life beat you down. My only brother, Tony, was willing to constantly coach and encourage his much younger brother to aim high. My sisters, Lynne, Helen, and Edna all had a significant impact on me. My children, Carrie, Mitchell and his wife, Kaley, and Kevin and Laura have challenged me, inspired me, and continue to bring me hope every day. I am blessed to have grandchildren, Micah, Hannah, and Avery.

As always, thank you to my incredible wife, Irene, for her great suggestions on letter topics, for putting up with me as I entertained yet another special project, and for being my partner in everything. I would not be where I am in the world without her constant and complete loving support.

With gratitude,

Maynard

About the Authors

Maynard Webb is a forty-year veteran of the technology industry. An active leader in the technology and business community, Maynard serves as a board member, investor, philanthropist, and mentor to young entrepreneurs.

As the founder of the Webb Investment Network (WIN), a seed investment firm dedicated to nurturing entrepreneurs, Maynard brings his experience developing and leading high-growth companies. WIN provides its portfolio companies with mentorship and on-demand access to an affiliate network of industry experts.

Maynard is the co-founder of Everwise, an idea that grew out of his best-selling book, *Rebooting Work*. Everwise provides workplace mentoring solutions. Through a data-driven matching process, Everwise connects professionals with mentors who can help them succeed at every stage of their career.

He serves on the board at Salesforce, Visa, and Everwise. Previously, he was the chairman and CEO of LiveOps, a cloud-based call center with a community of twenty thousand agents, and chairman and chairman emeritus of Yahoo! Prior to LiveOps, he was the COO of eBay. Webb has also served on several public and private boards including Gartner (NYSE: IT), Niku (NASD: NIKU), Extensity (NASD: EXTN), Hyperion (NASD: HYSL), Peribit (acquired by Juniper Networks), Baynote, and AdMob (acquired by Google) where he was also one of the first investors.

In 2004, he and his wife created the Webb Family Foundation, which provides underprivileged, motivated young individuals access to quality education and supports individuals who are struggling against the odds to make a positive impact on the world through innovation and hard work.

Maynard lives in Silicon Valley with his wife, Irene.

Carlye Adler is an award-winning journalist and bestselling author. Her writing has been published in *Businessweek, Fast Company, Fortune, Forbes, Newsweek, TIME,* and *Wired.* She has collaborated on four *New York Times* bestsellers: *Meditation for Fidgety Skeptics* by Dan Harris and Jeff Warren; *The Promise of a Pencil* by Adam Braun; *The Hard Thing About Hard Things* by Ben Horowitz and *Rebooting Work* by Maynard Webb. She is the coauthor of the national bestseller *Behind the Cloud* and *The Business of Changing the World* by Salesforce CEO Marc Benioff. She is also a coauthor with Jennifer Aaker and Andy Smith of *The Dragonfly Effect, Startupland* by Mikkel Svane. Her books have been translated into more than a dozen languages. She lives in Connecticut with her husband, two daughters, and a skateboarding bulldog.

Index